REFORMATION IN THE HOUSE

An Apostolic Model for the 21st Century Church

Bishop Tudor Bismark

Published by Truebrand Marketing Group
820 South MacArthur Blvd., Suite 105-301
Coppell, Texas 75019
www.truebrandpublishing.com

All Scripture quotations are taken from *The King James Version* of the Bible. Public Domain.

Content Development: Gary Wilde

ISBN   0-9725533-4-7
Printed in the United States of America

To Chi Chi, our Boys, the leadership of New Life Covenant Church in Harare, Zimbabwe, and to the Leaders of Jabula in the many countries we have ministry functions. Your willingness to submit to the teachings of Apostolic Government, and to allow the process of the Kingdom of God to be manifest has been a blessing to all. And to my Dad, Mom, brothers and sisters who believe in me and have given our anointing space. God bless you all.

Author's Note

As you read this book you will notice many references to types, symbols, and Biblical numerology. The Bible is written in metaphorical as well as literal language and in studying the types, symbols, and numbers one can gain a more thorough understanding of the message in each verse, chapter, book, and Bible as a whole. I encourage you to study the "hidden" truths throughout the Bible and would direct you to three books that have been instrumental in my own study: *Interpreting the Scriptures* and *Types and Symbols* by Kevin Conner, and *Dispensational Truths* by Larken.

CONTENTS

INTRODUCTION

IT'S ALL ABOUT THE HOUSE

Why does the blessing of God rest in certain places and not in other places? Why are some church leaders more favored than others? And why does God's anointing flow on one side of the road and yet, right across the street, there is no power, no fruit for the Kingdom?

These are hard questions. And some would say the fullest answers are rather complex. After all, we all call upon the same omnipotent Lord. However, I believe the most foundational answer is, in reality, quite simple: God always blesses apostolic ministry.

In this book, I invite you to delve into that answer in all of its many aspects. We'll explore the testimony of Scripture as we bring this answer to bear upon church health and growth. And yes, we're going to find that our answers are firmly grounded in the qualities of the apostle and the ministry of apostolic houses.

As we push deeper into these truths, we'll constantly be asking: What are the underlying common denominators telling us why God is blessing in certain places? In other words, if God is blessing a certain church in Harare, and a certain church in Dallas, and one in Kiev — do those three churches share factors making their blessing assured? If so, can we implement these things in places where God seems to withhold blessing? And can these factors, once implemented, transform communities, and then cities, and then entire nations?

Such exciting possibilities! I hope you are inspired by these questions to move ahead in this exploration with me. Because I do want to take you by the hand and show you all the power and potential of apostolic houses.

One of the first things we'll need to do, of course, is define the word apostolic. We'll go into this in detail later, but here I'd just like to say that it refers, generally, to anything built upon an apostle or apostolic team (based on the descriptions in the Book of Acts). Apostolic ministry seeks to transform cities and nations as the power of God is released through apostolic houses. These houses stand upon a five-fold ministry of apostles, prophets, evangelists, pastors, and teachers, in that order. This sets up a governmental order in which apostles become the legal conduits through whom God releases revelation, wisdom, and understanding. *(See Appendix #3 on page 145.)*

This is no pipe dream. God is at this moment blessing teams of apostles, not just in a particular church setting, but throughout cities and also within whole nations. Once the team of apostles begins working together, they transcend denominations, cultures, and social structures. In this transcending they bring a tremendous release of God's power.

One of the big reasons is this: The natural apostolic leadership of the body of Christ is rising up to assume its responsibility. Therefore we're seeing the enemy, the demonic princes, being matched rank on rank. It's an unprecedented anointing, releasing the supernatural. Isn't this what we all long to see?

But what, exactly, is the process of recognizing and building strong ministries on a five-fold basis? This is where the common denominators come into play — all of them making up the content of the chapters to follow. You see, successful ministries display a number of factors that prepare them for success in the 21st century.

Houses: Keys to Success

You can begin digging into these factors by thinking about five houses, which the Bible deals with throughout its pages. These are the five metamorphic processes of an apostolic house, each with its specific headship entity. Here's a quick, introductory overview of their basic characteristics: *(See Appendix #4 on page 146.)*

House #1: The individual.

According to Paul, in 1 Thessalonians 5:23, a human being consists of three parts: spirit, soul, and body. Because each body must have a head, this same biblical writer recommends, in Galatians 5, that we walk in the Spirit. If we walk in the Spirit, we will then be fulfilling the works of the Spirit. So the head of the first house, then, should be the Holy Spirit, who influences our human spirit.

Is this true in your own life? Is it how you live? If the Spirit is not leading you, the individual house, then you will have some serious problems accomplishing God's will in your world. You will have a soulless realm if the soul leads the house. You will have an appetite-driven house, or a sensory-driven house, if the body leads it.

House #2: The family

Again, we find three parts, and God's order and preference is: husband, wife, children. God has always emphasized the importance of family. If the man takes his rightful place as the priest of the house, and leads in governmental and spiritual leadership, that house will be in order and remain in order. No weapon against that house can prosper. But if the wife rules the house, then you've set up a matriarchal system, a disorder and a misappropriation of God's preference. Then the children, which are the next generation, will grow up in the wrong kind of environment. Of course (and I'm sure you've observed this!), if children rule the house . . . get ready for chaos.

House #3: The local church

I realize that for every particular local church, there's typically a different form of administration. But I am calling for unity in one aspect here. You see, most churches founded by a particular man or woman will have an apostolic anointing. So I recommend that a local church should have a single leader of that house which, for purposes of this book, will be called the set man. The anointing of that apostle, out of his particular spiritual loins, will then produce the success of that house.

Immediately beneath him that apostolic leader will oversee a governmental structure or an administration. And these will naturally differ in various cultures, in various nations, and in various styles of church leadership.

In our local church, I am the apostle, the set man. In our understanding of the Scripture, we then have an eldership, a board of deacons, and then various ministry leaders who function in particular ways. These will be defined later, but for now, see how this can look in chart form: *(See Appendix #2 on page 169.)*

Consider Dr. Cho and his church in South Korea. Here is an apostle with a series of pastoral leaders who have an apostolic mandate and anointing on their individual lives. That church has grown to over a million members. They have over fifty thousand individual leaders working in various ministries. It's an incredible church.

In China, the believers thrive under the Pentecostal house churches, which have a completely different kind of administration. There's an apostolic leader at the top, with thousands of individual house groups meeting under pastoral leaders. It's very successful and growing, with almost sixty million people in their church.

Cho's church? The house church? Which one is right? They're both right. They look different; they function according to their cultures. But they are both carrying out apostolic ministry.

I attended a church in Oakland, California, and met there apostles from Indonesia, India, and China. Each of these leaders employed a very different administrative style, but each of them was enjoying success in reaching his nation. They were all "right" in their styles.

There's an interesting style in Nigeria, within the Redeemed Christian Church of God. They have this philosophy: In Lagos, a huge city of thirteen million people (with 50 percent Muslim), you must not walk more than five minutes without being in the vicinity of a Redeemed Church. As a result, more than two million people worship in the Redeemed Christian Church there. When they get together at their once-a-month prayer meeting, they gather over a million people. Their administration type is very different, though, from what you might see in South Korea or China. But the successful local churches are apostolic in headship.

House #4: The local extension ministry.

Under God's blessing, a local church will extend itself to produce reproducing churches. In this situation, the father of the house will sire sons, and out of that particular house come sons who will start individual churches themselves. Then these churches may start churches, and those churches may start churches, until you have third- and fourth-generation churches under the auspices and direction of one original local church. That's how New Life

Ministries (or Jabula International Ministries) our ministry is structured. We have churches in fourteen different countries that have apostolic houses in their own right.

House #5: The corporate Kingdom of God.

Here we encounter our greatest challenge. A man or a woman may be a general in their own house, if they have significant numbers in their local church. But when they come into the corporate Kingdom of God on a national scale, they may not even be ranked as a corporal in that house. Because the Bible says when you come into the house of a strong man, don't take the high seat, take the low seat. If you take the high seat, estimating what your rank is, then when you leave your house as a general, and you come into somebody else's house, in that house you might be ranked as a corporal. And so you might have to be demoted in the corporate Kingdom of God! This is where we have some of our greatest challenges, but this is where God is moving in the greatest way. It is the movement of the Kingdom to take authority, not only in the home, in the local church, and in the city, but in the entire nation.

As we begin developing these particular chapters of apostolic houses, you'll begin seeing how they fit in God's conglomerate, His Kingdom. But please remem-ber: Some ministries have apostolic leaders who can literally build the apostolic house, but can't teach it. Some can teach the apostolic house, but can't build it. And there are those who can neither build it nor teach it, and those God has blessed to both build it and teach it. I want to establish here at the very beginning that those who build the apostolic house and teach the apostolic house are going to be the answer for success in the body of Christ.

The church is moving very quickly into the Acts 15 model of apostolic councils and apostolic roundtables, where conferences are going to be filled with dialogue. Out of this will come Spirit-led government and order. There will be proving and reforming doctrine, as well, so that the church becomes a place for correction.

The church is also going to be a place of restoration, because restoration must precede world revival.

A Restoration Is Coming!

In the Book of Acts, the Scripture speaks of a full restoration.

> *Repent ye therefore, and be converted, that your sins may be blotted out, when the times of refreshing shall come from the presence of the Lord; and he shall send Jesus Christ, which before was preached unto you: Whom the heaven must receive until the times of restitution of all things, which God hath spoken by the mouth of all his holy prophets since the world began.*
> —Acts 3:19-21

This "restitution" doesn't just include the restoration of New Testament things lost. No, it goes back to what was lost from the beginning, from what Adam lost, from what was lost even in the pre-Edenic world. This is where everything that was lost to a Satanic kingdom — all that was God's original intention for the church — will be restored by God.

Some things we didn't even know were lost! God is going to restore them. If you don't know what was lost, and God begins to restore it, you could find yourself in a very difficult position. If something is given to you, something you didn't know was lost in the first place, you may reject it. So we need councils where we can discuss with maturity the things God is bringing back. We'll need to dialogue about doctrinal positions and talk about what kinds of nations and governments God is raising. Just as an example: It's clear that God is going to restore the role of women in the church, some of whom are thoroughly rejected in various parts of the world.

In light of this coming restoration, what shall we do? The writer of Hebrews points the way:

> *Wherefore, holy brethren, partakers of the heavenly calling, consider the Apostle and High Priest of our profession,*

Christ Jesus; Who was faithful to him that appointed him, as also Moses was faithful in all his house. For this man was counted worthy of more glory than Moses, inasmuch as he who hath builded the house hath more honour than the house. For every house is builded by some man; but he that built all things is God. And Moses verily was faithful in all his house, as a servant, for a testimony of those things which were to be spoken after; but Christ as a son over his own house; whose house are we, if we hold fast the confidence and the rejoicing of the hope firm unto the end.

—Hebrews 3:1-6

We are to consider the faithfulness of our great Apostle, Jesus Christ . . . and hold fast. The theme here is better things — a better Savior, a better covenant, a better sacrifice, a better . . . everything. The old system of Moses was great, but a better system is coming, a system built on the foundation of Apostle Jesus, who built an incredible house, indeed.

Jesus said the wise man builds his house upon the rock. In this book you'll explore the building of that particular house. Here are some of the themes to come:

♦ recognizing the characteristics of an apostle;

♦ discerning whether or not you have an apostolic house;

♦ understanding governmental authority;

♦ growing as a house of deliverance;

♦ nurturing intercessory prayer among your members;

♦ witnessing the power of an open heaven;

♦ knowing, and using, your measure of rule;

♦ proclaiming the authenticity of God's house.

We're also going to discuss the transforming of nations, starting with the transformation of a community. Finally, in an extended Appendix section, I've included a fully outlined description of key Old Testament apostolic models, laying out both their strengths and weaknesses for your personal instruction and growth.

Ready to Play Your Part?

Philosopher and art critic John Ruskin once said: "If you do not wish God's kingdom, don't pray for it. But if you do, you must do more than pray for it; you must work for it."

It's a stirring thought, made even more poignant when we know this man's interesting history. Raised in an evangelical home, he grew into adulthood ques-tioning everything. As a young man he suffered terribly with doubt, with horrific nightmares and depression, even lapsing into periods that might be called insanity. After fully renouncing Christianity during those days, he could never quite give up on the hope of a better place, a kingdom to come. His life on earth was so tortured; he felt he had to at least believe in some kind of afterlife. As he approached his closing years, he returned to his Christian faith. God never let go of Ruskin and, in the end, this man trusted Christ for salvation. But for him, "Thy Kingdom come" was a great struggle, an internal battle of epic proportions.

Really, is it so different for any of us? We are saved by grace, but if we wish the Kingdom to come in our homes and cities and nations we must pray and work. For we are here to be the hands and feet of our Savior, the almighty One who will return one day to restore perfectly what we can only faithfully work to restore imperfectly, as best we can, in the meantime.

I know you can relate to such a journey of faith. We all sometimes struggle — yes, even with doubt, sickness, and depression. But the call to us is the same as the one proclaimed to every human being who has ever lived: Look to the Kingdom for abundant life.

If it is not enough only to pray for that Kingdom, then each one of us must ask ourselves daily, with our hearts open to God: "What, dear Lord, is my part to play? Were am I called to serve? Where am I asked to lead? And how shall I start, this very day?"

As you trust God to lead you, take your first step. Read the chapters ahead. Learn more about the Kingdom, and let this book be an encouragement to you. As you move through its pages, do so with a prayerful and seeking heart. I know God will answer in the most marvelous ways as you say: "Use me, Holy Spirit!"

— *Bishop Tudor Bismark*
  Summer 2004

1

COULD YOU RECOGNIZE A REAL APOSTLE?

We all know about the original apostles, those who were with Jesus. And we do well to admire them and hold them up as examples — not only in their manner of life, but also in their courage at life's end. For example, tradition holds that those apostles died in the following ways:[i]

♦ Matthew suffered martyrdom by being slain with a sword in a city of Ethiopia.

♦ Mark expired at Alexandria, after being cruelly dragged through the streets.

♦ Luke was hanged on an olive tree in Greece.

♦ John was put in a caldron of boiling oil, but escaped death miraculously before he was banished to Patmos.

♦ Peter was crucified, upside-down at Rome.

♦ James, the Greater, was beheaded at Jerusalem.

◆ James, the Less, was thrown from a pinnacle of the temple, and then beaten to death with a club.

◆ Bartholomew was flayed alive.

◆ Andrew was bound to a cross, and preached to his persecutors until he died.

◆ Thomas was run through the body with a lance in the East Indies.

◆ Jude was shot to death with arrows.

◆ Matthais was first stoned and then beheaded.

Clearly, the call to apostleship should never be taken lightly! It is serious business — and definitely risky.

We honor the apostles past while recognizing that the position and role of apostleship is not over. We are to have apostles in the church today, but we must know what they are and what they do. They should certainly be persons of high character and complete dedication to the Lord, just as their earliest exemplars were. But let's look closer at the modern-day ideal.

Defining "Apostle" and the Apostolic Role

The basic definition of apostle, based upon the meaning of the original Greek Bible word is simply: "Sent one" or "messenger." In the New Testament, the word refers particularly to the twelve men whom Jesus selected to be with him and whom he sent out to preach and to cast out demons *(see Mark 3:14-15)*. But indi-viduals other than the Twelve bore that title as well *(for example, Paul and Barnabas; Acts 14:14)*. Apostles were appointed by Christ, not by men *(see Galatians 1:1)*, and they gave authoritative witness to what God had done in Christ *(see Acts 1:22)*.[ii]

This is a basic definition, but we can expand upon it. An apostle, as a sent one, is a man or a woman whom God has anointed with the mandate of a trailblazer. An apostle's house, then, is a church or a ministry where an anointed man or woman produces the following fruit:

♦ They are pioneers who produce kingdom-building strategies, not just for a church but for a region, not just for a city but for cities, not just for a nation but for nations.

♦ They also produce vision, policy, structure, government, direction, correction, and order.

♦ They are a life source, producing not just physical healing but spiritual healing — not just opening physically blind eyes, but also opening spiritually blind eyes.

♦ They raise the dead wherever life has ceased, resurrecting dead ministries, dead visions, dead churches.

These apostolic ministries produce Kingdom administration, and Kingdom rule. They are actually the new church order, which has come to pass after the post-denominational era. In this new order we see towns and villages, cities and communities, nations and ethnic groups, which were once bound by Satanic rule, now bowing to truth when an apostolic rank comes into rule. Demonic powers are matched, rank-to-rank with ministry. And this ministry proceeds with anointing by the Holy Spirit, all for the purpose of national transfor-mation that honors Christ and His Kingdom.

The apostle's role, then, is to bring revelation, deli-verance, healing, the removing of demonic spirits — not just out of individuals, but out of entire communities, along streets, in suburbs, in cities, amidst entire provinces, even across nations where devils must be removed. An apostle's role is to release captives, break chains of bondage, unfold mysteries of the time, reveal secrets, and crown ministries with new authority.

God also calls apostles to open the heavens over nations, over cities, and over local churches. They are to shut the gates of hell, break the spirits of witchcraft, destroy curses and illegal covenants. They are to restore order, and maintain and restore the rights of believers. They are to unfold and distribute inheritances. They are to lead God's people away from Egypt and lead them into the spiritual promised land where God's Kingdom is to be established.

When we discuss the role of the apostle and the role of apostolic houses, we also have to look closely at the divine mandate. God gives different mandates to fulfill an entire picture, so to speak. So within a city where you have hundreds of churches, God may raise up a handful of apostolic houses to bring down demonic structure and demonic order. Here I think of the words of Hebrews 3:1-6:

> *Wherefore, holy brethren, partakers of the heavenly calling, consider the Apostle and High Priest of our profession, Christ Jesus; Who was faithful to him that appointed him, as also Moses was faithful in all his house.*
>
> *For this man was counted worthy of more glory than Moses, inasmuch as he who hath builded the house hath more honour than the house. For every house is builded by some man; but he that built all things is God.*
>
> *And Moses verily was faithful in all his house, as a servant, for a testimony of those things which were to be spoken after; But Christ as a son over his own house; whose house are we, if we hold fast the confidence and the rejoicing of the hope firm unto the end.*

Jesus built his house. By structuring his house, he was then able to break the rule of Satan and establish a Kingdom that has no end. When the writer uses Moses as an example, he shows us what Moses accomplished and attained through the anointing on his life.

So we see that an apostle is also a house, or a ministry. We find the earliest roots of this emphasis in many of the things God hinted at in the Old Testament. We can observe some examples by quickly surveying five Old Testament personalities and summarizing their key qualities.

Abraham: *Covenanting in Ministry*

God made a covenant with Abraham, promising him land, seed, and blessing. A portion of that promise reads like this:

> And [God] brought [Abraham] forth abroad, and said, Look now toward heaven, and tell the stars, if thou be able to number them: and he said unto him, So shall thy seed be. And he believed in the Lord; and he counted it to him for righteousness. And he said unto him, I am the Lord that brought thee out of Ur of the Chaldees, to give thee this land to inherit it.
>
> And he said, Lord God, whereby shall I know that I shall inherit it?
>
> —Genesis 15:5-8

Even though he believed, Abraham still wondered about something. He asked the Lord, "How am I going to inherit the blessing you promised?" The Lord then tells him to make a sacrifice:

first, a heifer;

second, a she-goat;

third, a ram;

fourth, a turtledove;

fifth, a pigeon.

I believe all of these particular animals have representative characteristics alluding to fivefold ministry. The heifer was the apostle. It was to be sacrificed in order to open the doors for sins to be forgiven. This heifer was given an anointing to produce the next generation. So when Abraham sacrificed it, it then became the apostle.

The she-goat, then, was the prophet. It had the ability to produce the milk that would bring life for the sacrifice of atonement. Remember that in the sacrifices under the Aaronic order, priests were to bring twin goats, one to be slain, it's blood sprinkled on the altar. But the high priest would lay his hands on the second goat and pronounce the sins of the nation upon it. Then it would be let go, as a 'scapegoat," into the wilderness. This spoke of a prophetic utterance that was to come.

The ram was the evangelist. It produced the seed, and that seed was to go into a new ground to produce the lambs that were coming into the Kingdom, because we are his sheep and we are the lambs of his pasture.

Then the turtledove, which was a very gentle creature, speaks of the role of the pastor, a gentle shepherd. The turtledove was to exemplify love.

Finally, the young pigeon was a creature that could fly. It could carry a message to remote parts of the earth. It has a powerful homing instinct: If it is released in any part of the earth, it will find its way back. So the teacher, the pigeon, then, can search its way through the Scriptures and find its way home. Thus Abraham shows us the fivefold ministry in entering into covenant with God. In this covenant, his question is answered, his inheritance is sure.

> *KEY QUALITY: APOSTLES STAY FAITHFUL IN THEIR COVENANT WITH GOD, SETTING UP AND OVERSEEING A FIVEFOLD MINISTRY.*

Aaron, Nadab, Abihu: *Warning against Apostasy*

Aaron was priest over Israel and also provides a hint of the fivefold ministry to come. In his role, he became the apostle. Because he was the founder, the builder of what was to now become the Jewish worship system. Nadab was the prophet. Abihu was the evangelist. Eliezer was the pastor. Ithamar became the teacher.

The names of each of these men speak of certain things. When I look at the meanings of their Hebrew names, I see a congruency with their roles:

♦ **Apostle Aaron**: meaning *mountain of strength* (speaks of a high place of leadership and authority);

♦ **Prophet Nadab**: meaning *Of one's free will* or *generous* (speaks of the liberal spreading of God's Word, preaching God's vision, far and wide);

♦ **Evangelist Abihu**: meaning *He is my father* (speaks of the basic content of Gospel preaching: God, our Father, with Jesus His Son);

♦ **Pastor Eliezer**: meaning *Help of God* (speaks of God's shepherding and helping care);

♦ **Teacher Ithamar**: meaning *Palm tree* or *Palm island* (speaks of a place of retreat for learning; teachers in those days often sat under trees to teach their students).

It is noteworthy here that Nadab and Abihu messed up. They offered "strange fire" (i.e., common fire that wasn't taken from the great brazen altar, as God had instructed), so God destroyed them *(see Lev. 6:9; 10:1-2)*. Why? Because prophets and evangelists have the propensity to offer wild fire more than any of the other ministers. They must be careful not to get carried away in the moment. They must beware letting emotional electricity replace doctrinal purity.

KEY QUALITY: *APOSTLES RECEIVE AND TEACH THE TRUTH — MAKING SURE THE OTHER MINISTERS CONFORM TO RIGHT DOCTRINE, AS WELL.*

David: *Fighting Kingdom Battles*

David killed Goliath, the giant Philistine. The Bible says this courageous young man took five stones out of the brook to face a mammoth man who had armor, sword and spear. But when David took those five stones out of the brook, he took the fivefold ministry. When he shot the first stone, it was the apostle that killed the giant. The first stone represented the apostle, and if the giant hadn't fallen, the rest of the stones would have made it happen.

A group of historians compiled this startling information: Since 3600 B.C., the world has known only 292 years of peace! During this period there have been 14,351 wars, in which 3.64 billion people have been killed. The value of the property destroyed is equal to a golden belt around the world 97.2 miles wide and 33 feet thick. Since 650 B.C., there have also been 1,656 arms races, only 16 of which have not ended in war. The remainder ended in the economic collapse of the countries involved.[iii]

Here's my point: Never forget that each of us believers is fighting a cosmic battle daily. It's a war that never ceases until the Day of the Lord. We don't have 292 years of no warfare. We don't even have a single day away from this conflict while we breathe here on earth.

The Kingdom battle rages, every minute of every day, since Lucifer first rebelled with his cohort of angels in heaven. Since that time, even after Christ won back the world, Satan tries to destroy all that God created — especially his new creatures in Christ. Apostles fight this battle with faith and prayer and fasting . . . and with each pebble the Lord provides.

> **KEY QUALITY:** *APOSTLES ARE POWERFUL, COURAGEOUS WARRIORS IN KINGDOM BATTLES, FIGHTING WITH GREAT FAITH, EVEN WHEN RESOURCES ARE SCARCE.*

Zechariah: *Building with Broad Understanding*

Zechariah was a prophet appearing on the scene sixteen years after the seventy-year exile of the Israelites in Babylon. He was mentored by prophet Haggai, and you can read both of their books in the Bible.

The main thrust of Zechariah's message to the children of Israel was: "You're not doing well because the house of God lies unfinished. You ignore God's house while continuing to build your own houses. Wrong! You must complete the house of God!"

In Zechariah 1, he said he saw four forces ("horns") that destroy the house of God and scatter what God had established. He then saw four craftsmen, or "workers with hammers" (the King James Version calls them "carpenters"), and these four come to build up what the four powers had destroyed.

Here again was the fivefold ministry. Why do I say this? Because if you are going to be an apostle, you must have an understanding of the prophetic, the evan-gelistic, the pastor, and the teacher roles. You see, if a man is going to be an architect designing buildings, he must understand all the major disciplines in con-struction: bricklaying, plumbing, carpentry, etc. But the bricklayer doesn't have to understand plumbing; the plumber doesn't need to understand carpentry; the carpenter doesn't have to understand bricklaying.

Similarly, a teacher doesn't necessarily have to be an apostle, as long as he's a teacher, and so on. But if you are going to be an apostle, you have to be able to preach (be a prophet), evangelize, pastor, and teach. Not all pastors are apostles. Not all prophets are apostles. Not all teachers are apostles. But if a man is to be an architect of the house, he must understand all of the building disciplines. So Zechariah, when he saw these four craftsmen, actually saw the four major disciplines: prophets, evangelists, pastors and teachers. Knowing those four was to walk in the role of an apostle.

> **KEY QUALITY:** *APOSTLES HAVE BROAD UNDERSTANDING OF MINISTRY PRINCIPLES AND KNOW HOW TO BUILD THE KINGDOM WORK, STEP BY STEP, CONSTANTLY DEPENDING ON GOD'S GUIDANCE.*

Jethro and Moses: *Knowing How to Delegate*

When Moses was banished from Israel after he killed an Egyptian, he went to the house of Midian, where Jethro (also called Reuel) was priest. Jethro had seven daughters, and Moses married one of them: Zipporah. He then settled down with Jethro and received training to be an apostle . . . raising sheep! As lowly as the job was, Moses nevertheless began to understand what God is calling him to be: a deliverer of His people.

When Moses eventually delivered the children of Israel out of the land of slavery, and they entered the wilderness on their way to the Promised Land, Jethro then came and gave Moses a deeper understanding of what his role was to be. He basically said, "Moses, you are an apostle, or a leader, and you yourself must stick close to God. Don't allow all these petty little problems in the camp to distract you from your true leadership role. Here's what you should do, Moses: set up captains of tens, of fifties, of hundreds, and of thousands. Then your ministry will function as God intends."

Moses took his father-in-law's advice. Thus God shows us the wisdom of a definite pattern of leadership in the Scriptures.

KEY QUALITY: THE APOSTLE FOLLOWS WISE AND GOD-ORDAINED PATTERNS OF LEADERSHIP, BEING ESPECIALLY SKILLFUL AT DELEGATING RESPONSIBILITIES ACCORDING TO PEOPLES' GIFTS.

Can you see, then, that throughout the Old Testament God hints at what's coming in apostolic ministry? Since Moses' learning (about delegating) is so important, we need to break it down and apply it to the church today.

Crucial Characteristics of Captains

One problem in the church today is that too many small leaders are trying to be big leaders. Conversely, so many who are called to be big leaders are not coming to the front and assuming their responsibility. When Jethro gave this plan in Exodus 18, it was endorsed by God in Deuteronomy 1:15. It was also endorsed and implemented in David's structure in 1 Chronicles 13:1. It was further endorsed and implemented by Solomon in 2 Chronicles 1:2. Therefore, let's not be afraid of doing things this way — God's way!

Be clear about what Jethro taught us. When we have ranks in apostolic ministries, we will find that the captains of Ten's will have certain characteristics that differ from the others. Because not everybody who is a Captain of Tens has the ability to do what Captains of Thousands can do (though both roles are important to the Kingdom's progress).

Now for a specific look at captain's characteristics before closing out this chapter. [**Note:** I'll use "he" for these descriptions, but please realize that women also carry out apostolic ministry.]

The Captain of Tens:

♦ The father of an extended family, of a basic assembly that is built on relationships and close fellowship.

♦ This man doesn't have a broad-ranging, dynamic public ministry. He works more on a one-to-one basis.

♦ He knows the Scripture, but he imparts it in a conversational way.

♦ His main gift is pastoral, so he loves people, and he loves to spend time with them.

♦ His life is an example to others. Follow him as he follows Christ.

♦ He does not necessarily initiate strategy, but he's loyal to those who do initiate. Sometimes he's the kind of person who goes from conference to conference looking for new ideas. He imparts and applies those ideas in a limited way because his mind is closed to the broader outreach. He is mainly a traditional, orthodox kind of leader.

♦ His basic gift is that of an encourager. He is an exalter rather than a preacher, and he speaks positively of leadership that is more gifted.

♦ He can work to a maximum of maybe 40–50 people. This person's church will not grow more than 75.

The Captain of Fifties:

♦ Also the father of an extended family who loves people, enjoys working with them individually, and works at remembering people's names.

♦ He can teach publicly and often uses parables to convey biblical truths.

♦ He has some organizational skill; however, he still does most everything himself: driving the church bus, setting up chairs, fixing the PA system. In the service, he will open in prayer, lead the songs, take up the offering. He baptizes everybody, dedicates every baby, officiates at every wedding and funeral, and stands by every hospital bed.

♦ He concentrates on Christian living as opposed to strategy. Therefore, he does not initiate strategy. If he's honest, would tell you that he prefers working under someone else in authority. When he gets a new idea, applies that idea in a limited way.

♦ He does not know how to develop leaders by identifying their gifts. In fact, he's struggling to develop himself.

♦ Men of greater gift love this kind of man because he's a hard worker and a soul winner. He can be developed into what I would call a "set man."

♦ This person, even though he has some organizational skill, will never have a national impact or even a citywide impact. He ministers only his local assembly.

◆ His church won't grow much beyond 150 people, because when he starts getting more gifted people coming to his church, they tend to intimidate him rather than motivate him. (In a sense, they become a curse, not a blessing.)

The Captain of Hundreds:

◆ This kind of man clearly has ability for public ministry. He can speak well, giving them biblical meat to take home.

◆ He has good organizational ability. He tends to delegate but doesn't produce leaders; instead, he produces helpers. In his departments, they are still depending on strategy, leadership, and instruction from him. He has a plurality of leadership but most of the leadership are helpers.

◆ His vision tends to be primarily local. It's not extended into a nation. Small provisions for small national things will be at all kinds of national meetings in a very insignificant way.

◆ His primary gift is pastoral, though he can be prophetic and tends to be very evangelistic. He will organize chicken dinners, handing out sweets; street services, knocking on doors. But he rarely has a major impact in a particular community.

◆ He can develop into a set man or into an apostolic leader, but he's going to struggle because he doesn't read enough to get enough information. He doesn't have men of greater gifts to take him to the next level, because these people intimidate him.

◆ He can handle between 150–400 adults very well and will probably lead a church of about 600.

The Captain of Thousands:

◆ These are the true apostles who change nations. God has gifted them for great works.

◆ He has an effective public preaching ministry. The larger the crowd, the better he ministers. His preaching will draw people from miles around. He holds people when he ministers, mesmerizes them with the anointing.

◆ He knows how to lead men. He inspires them and releases men of greater gift. In fact, men of greater gifts will flock around this kind of person because he's an inspirational, motivational leader.

◆ He keeps his finger on everything, but is not interested in details. He releases areas of responsibility. For example, he directs counseling to other people. He prefers to work with other leaders and not with people in his ministry or in his church. He doesn't like going to hospitals, doesn't like going to baby dedications, doesn't like spending time at people's weddings. His main focus is developing leaders.

◆ He is mostly concerned with vision and strategy, and with spotting gifted people who can develop and release leadership (think of Paul and Timothy). He is able to release his pulpit, release his gift to men of other gifts, so that their gifts can be on display without being intimidated by the diversity of their gifts.

◆ He is able to inspire gifted men and make them even bigger and even greater than they are.

◆ He can work submissively around other captains of 1000's and can help motivate them as they help motivate him.

◆ This individual is strong enough to bring correction to other leaders who step out of line. He will not tolerate disloyalty in the ranks but will also encourage men of lesser gift to bring greater vision to the bigger picture.

◆ The early years of this man's ministry tend to be filled with turbulence and frustration, tests and trials. God is preparing him for great responsibility.

* * * *

So . . . can you recognize an apostle when you see one? Can you recognize the kinds of captains God uses? And which kind are you? All these forms of apostolic ministry are valuable and needed in the Kingdom. Why not pause right now and pray that God will use you to your fullest potential?

2

YOUR MOST IMPORTANT TOP TWENTY!

Do you know the difference between a boss and a leader? Consider:

√ a boss creates fear; A LEADER CREATES CONFIDENCE.

√ a boss creates resentment; A LEADER BREEDS ENTHUSIASM.

√ a boss says, "I"; A LEADER SAYS, "WE".

√ a boss fixes blame; A LEADER FIXES MISTAKES.

√ a boss *knows* how; A LEADER *SHOWS* HOW.

√ a boss makes work drudgery; A LEADER MAKES WORK INTERESTING.

√ a boss relies on authority; A LEADER RELIES ON COOPERATION.

√ a boss drives; A LEADER LEADS.

Apostles are the leaders of the church. They have authority in the local assembly, of course; but they use it wisely and for the good of all. Furthermore, anointed apostles make up the corporate team for a ministry that expands far beyond the local church. But to develop an apostolic team, the apostle himself must be developed.

Apostolic Leaders: What Must They Have?

We've already looked at the definition and roles of the apostle in our previous chapter. We were speaking in general terms there; now we're ready to speak in specific terms about personal requirements. You see, if an apostolic leader is not developed as an individual, then immaturity will be a problem, especially when the difficult times come. So the apostolic leader must have certain disciplines and certain belief systems.

There are many of these important requirements. This chapter, in fact, could consist of scores of lists. However, I've narrowed down the requirements to only one score — to an absolutely essential Top Twenty List. As David Letterman does with his nightly Top Ten, let's start at the bottom and move to the top of our list together. Here's what an apostle must have in building himself and his team . . .

#20 *He must have an apostle's mouth.*

That is, he needs a fine-tuned voice of strategy, one that can mobilize people at any given moment. For example, if an apostle calls for prayer, people quickly mobilize around prayer. If he says we need to take a special offering, they mobilize around that offering. If he says we should fast, people mobilize around a fast. The apostle's mouth becomes a fine-tuned trumpet, a call to action in the Kingdom.

#19 *He must be able to take an offering.*

A work needs to be done, and an apostle will need to ask for the money. The Bible says the apostles took offerings that came to their feet. Now, this is over and above general offerings and tithes. In this case, the Lord will speak and say, "Take an offering and send it to Mozambique for the starving people." That is an apostolic offering, because people who give in that situation, receive a greater blessing than when giving to a general offering.

And, yes, an apostle himself must be willing to give in an apostle's offering. Certainly there are times when God will call an apostle to sow into another apostle's ministry. Sometimes you will even drain your church's finances in order to send money to another church.

#18 *He must actively school the young ones.*

Apostles are only human; they have a finite lifespan. They will rise, serve, and ebb. When an apostle comes into his time and releases his gifting, he must understand that when his lifespan of apostlehood wanes, someone else must be ready to take the lead. He'll always be an apostle, but as he gets older and his role changes, he must mentor the ones who are rising.

This is where the "school of the apostle" is so helpful. In many places apostolic leaders are now mentoring and training new leaders to be released decades from now into their roles.

Yet, why are so few doing this kind of mentoring? So many times, apostolic leaders have to be mentored by what I call "remote control" — by watching and observing from a distance, by reading, watching videos, and trying to be around men with an apostolic mantle. I admire these young people. They just want to spend a few minutes with their apostolic leaders because it's often not possible to spend a few hours. But apostles must be mentored. Why not spend the hours?

#17 *He must practice the art of visualization.*

An apostle needs a clear eye to see what God is bringing in the future. If he can't do this, then he'll never build the people and the team, and he won't be ready for what's coming. For instance, if an apostle can visualize in the Spirit that difficult times loom ahead, then he can prepare the people, physically, mentally, and spiritually for perseverance. If God shows you that a famine is coming, you can store up food. If God shows you there's a bumper harvest coming, you can build bigger barns. That's the art of visualization.

And think about the power of words to form an image. Apostles must have this ability. God will sometimes send me to a place and I'll preach things so incredible that I'm thinking, *My God, where did that come from?* I find that I'm simply forming an image for those people in that region. Where we may feel as if a revival is impossible, the words of the apostle can form a different image — now it is possible!

I was preaching in Wales, and a group of men said to me: "You know, before this conference, we thought it was impossible to have big churches here. But after you painted the picture in four nights of preaching and teaching, we saw how it could happen. An African guy has come to Wales and painted us the big picture!" Visualize God's will, and use powerful words to form the image for others.

#16 *He must have a sense of apostolic timing.*

If an apostle comes late, he will miss the wave. And trying to chase the wave is a problem. Think in terms of surfing. If the apostle is on time, as the wave begins to crest, he's catching it, riding the momentum. Then the wave is doing all the work.

But if you're late, then you have to catch up with that wave. Hard work, indeed!

So an apostle needs to know the timing of God — not just when he is preaching, but in the entire essence of his ministry. We often call this "apostolic realignment." That is, when God reveals a new way — a new path to take — we have to be flexible and ready to adjust our vision and approach. What God showed us there in that ministry of the past, may differ from what he is saying here and now.

#15 *He must "be" what his people are to "become."*

As the head is, so becomes the body. So if the leader is blessed, the body is blessed. If the leader gets revelation, the body gets revelation.

We see this with Old Testament Aaron. The oil was poured on Aaron's head and ran all the way down his beard, all the way down his garments, all the way down to his feet. So, he becomes an apostolic type. As is with him, so is it with the rest of the body.

This has special application to the arts and worship. There are times when an apostle will release certain songs, certain music, lead in certain worship. That time of worship is not just to make people feel good; it will literally tear down strongholds.

#14 *He must have an apostolic awareness.*

This is about truly knowing where you are. You can be in strange surroundings with demonic forces and you might not know who your allies are. . . and who your allies are not. Yet if God wants you to go there and share your gift, you'll need to know how to share in a way that meets a specific type of hearer — and then get out!

#13 *He must speak with apostolic language.*

Apostles will say things in an apostolic way because of their emphasis on strategy and structure. We must understand that when we have apostolic mandates, God will cause us to speak prophetically. But it's not just prophetic, it is authoritative. Because sometimes we have a prophetic word that's a positional word, but an apostolic prophetic word is an authoritative word. That is, in his language the apostle can say, "The demonic influences in this area are judged, and they will die."

I've been in several places around the globe and felt the Spirit of God judge against demonic spirits in the area. I've called out witches and witchdoctors com-manding them to repent because God is offering them a specific opportunity, a season of repentance and if they don't accept it and repent their going to die. And on several occasions witches in the area have refused to repent and they have died.

Apostles use apostolic language — they can judge.

#12 *He must know how to fight in Spiritual warfare.*

Sometimes God will send a man or a woman as an apostle to a certain region in order to war against demonic spirits in prayer. Many times when I'm sent, I will just walk the streets of that city. I will call on God in those cities as if I'm in a battle. But sometimes God may not physically send you to an area with demonic strongholds. Sometimes you will wrestle with demonic strongholds in your spirit only. This is spiritual warfare.

In spiritual warfare, an apostle clearly needs a yoke-breaking anointing. How to get it? Take the words of Jesus to heart:

> *And when [Jesus] was come into the house, his disciples asked him privately, Why could not we cast him out?*

> *And he said unto them, This kind can come forth by nothing, but by prayer and fasting.*

> —Mark 9:28-29

#11 *He must honor apostolic protocol.*

We need to understand who's who in the body of Christ. We need to know who has the anointing to do certain things. Here's an example: Two years ago, we wanted to start all-night prayer meetings and invite the whole body of Christ in Harare to participate. So we had planned our date, and just as we were about to publicize it, I heard that Langton Gatsi, was having special meetings at the same time. This was a time for apostolic protocol.

We postponed our plans because I believe — and many others in this nation believe — that he is the apostle of prayer for this nation. So we just submitted to him, due to his rank and his calling. We must honor apostolic protocol.

#10 *He must be ready to admonish — and to be admonished.*

I'm talking about apostolic chastisement, and two things are important here. First, sometimes apostles must speak words of judgment. You may come across a ministry that is actually hindering the Kingdom of God. Then you'll need to say words like: "If you continue in the way you are going, God will surely replace you."

Second, sometimes individuals (including our-selves) may need to be chastised for irresponsible statements. As an apostle in the city, I can't just write something and put it in the newspaper without checking first with other men of God in the city. I could be bringing unnecessary hurt to the body of Christ. So if I'm going to say anything that might cause social unrest, I'd better make sure I've heard from God and all the other apostles in the city. If I've made a mistake, I must be willing to receive admonishment from others.

There are some things you don't need to check out with other apostles, of course. If there's violence in the city, you have to speak out against violence. You don't need to phone another man and discuss that. No, the Scripture is clear on those things. But if we start talking about coming against government policies and declaring our position, we'd better make sure we're clear with other people.

#9 *He must practice apostolic alchemy.*

The word alchemy includes the idea of "getting better in value," of transforming something common into something precious. There are times when an apostle is needed in a certain place to increase the value and credibility of that ministry. When the apostle releases the anointing in apostolic alchemy, the value of the pastor in the ministry he has anointed increases, and the value of his family increases as well. In fact, the value of all the leaders starts increasing, including the value of their property and their gifts. God opens doors, just because that apostle has come to release the gift.

#8 *He must eat apostolic food.*

Do you know what feeds your spirit? God will supply, so you can be fed. Elijah was told, "Eat, because your journey is long." Sometimes God will cause you to feed in certain pastures because of where you're going in your journey. Be open to the messages He sends to you.

In my office at home, I have barrels of audiotapes that I collect. Many of those tapes I've never had time to hear. But once in a while, when I'm rummaging through, I find a series of tapes and think, My God, I didn't know I had these! I'll spend a whole season listening to those, because they prepare me for the journey I'm about to take. I've got an unbelievable number of books, many of them I haven't yet had time to read. But lately I've been reading books on strategy and leadership and staffing, because this is the journey, the path God is leading me to take.

#7 *He must "live what's coming."*

This is the mindset of living now what you are going to enter into. It means walking in the anointing of what you are going to become in Christ. What could be better, for instance, than to live in the constant awareness that your life is with Christ in heaven? The biblical apostles can explain it better than I can, so I'll let their words suffice here:

> *Our citizenship is in heaven. And we eagerly await a Savior from there, the Lord Jesus Christ, who, by the power that enables him to bring everything under his control, will*

transform our lowly bodies so that they will be like his glorious body. —Philippians 3:20-21 (NIV)

If ye then be risen with Christ, seek those things which are above, where Christ sitteth on the right hand of God. Set your affection on things above, not on things on the earth. For ye are dead, and your life is hid with Christ in God.

—Colossians 3:1-3

For now we see through a glass, darkly; but then face to face: now I know in part; but then shall I know even as also I am known. —1 Corinthians 13:12

Beloved, now are we the sons of God, and it doth not yet appear what we shall be: but we know that, when he shall appear, we shall be like him; for we shall see him as he is.

—1 John 3:2

#6   *He must live by apostolic economics.*

God always finances genuine apostolic ministries. He will send gifted people with loads of money into the church. But if an apostle is not sharp, he might exploit people for the wrong things. He might abuse the funding process.

In our church, we are quite cautious here. We don't take special offerings for every single thing. We take offerings on Sunday. We trust God to fund valid, Spirit-led ministries, and you can do so, as well.

#5   *He must preserve himself and his ministry.*

Some apostles burn themselves out in a few years. Then they are not effective when they come to their real time for fruitful ministry. In my life, I try to eat right, especially when I am traveling. I eat one meal a day, exercise every day, and stay away from junk food. Because my best years are coming, I must preserve myself for them. I don't want to be in a wheelchair through any fault of my own! Our message must be preserved — and we must work at preserving the messenger.

#4 *He must pray, pray, pray.*

God will sometimes wake me up and I'll pray all night, sleep all day. So if you don't see me at the office, don't think, "This guy is lazy!" I was up all night! Sometimes an unusual anointing will come for apostolic intercession, not even for me or for the church, but for some strange place, and I must pray.

Prayer also plays a part in what I call the "push and pull" of the apostolic office. That is, we must pray when God is pulling an apostle into a region to do a work. Similarly, we must pray when the apostolic gift in a region must be pushed out to a certain area to do a certain work. Intercessors need to know whether God is pulling or pushing, or both.

#3 *He must walk in the highest integrity.*

There's nothing more disgusting than an apostle who doesn't walk in integrity. An apostle must be morally upright and walk in sexual purity. He must not compromise, maintaining strong convictions. Far in advance of temptation, he'll set firm, unbending boundaries. In all his relationships and financial dealings, he seeks to live above reproach.

#2 *He must write on his calendar — in pencil.*

Please, apostles, don't overbook yourselves! Write in pencil, because you might have to change your assignment. God works in mysterious ways. Let us be ready to move with Him.

Two Novembers ago the Lord spoke to me and told me to stay at home in November. I wanted to go to Jamaica, because I always go to Jamaica in November, but in obedience, I canceled the trip.

Then I sensed the Lord speaking to me: I'm going to bless you on the 17th of December. On that night, I dreamed of a building with four stories. The next day we went to look for that building . . . and we found it. It's now Jabula Heights our office building. But that wouldn't have happened if I was in Jamaica, if I'd refused to use my pencil — and my eraser. Apostles, your calendar must be written in pencil. You can be on your way to preach in Samaria, and God will tell you, "Go to Gaza and wait, because there's an Ethiopian coming" *(see Acts 8:26-40).*

#1   *He must stay a team player.*

We've now come full circle, back to the idea that opened this chapter: a leader is better than a boss. A leader can listen to the ideas of his team members without feeling threatened. He can rejoice in their successes without jealousy. He can guide and mentor and coach, all the while lavishing the kind of affirmation and love that he himself receives from the Lord.

Yes, a boss drives; a leader leads.

Are You Ready to Lead?

With all I've said about being a team player and the differences between bossing and leading, there is still an important "loner" aspect to the apostolic role. To be called to lead in the church means being placed in situations where you, and you alone, are God's man for the circumstances. Will you be ready?

E. Stanley Jones tells of a missionary who got lost in an African jungle. There was nothing around him but bush and a few cleared places. He found a hut and asked the man living there to lead the way out. The man living in the hut agreed to lead the missionary out of the bush.

"All right," said the missionary. "Show me the way."

The man said, "Walk."

So they walked and hacked their way through the unmarked jungle for more than an hour. The missionary got worried. "Are you quite sure this is the way? Where is the path?"

"In this place there is no path," the man said. "I am the path."

3

Is Your House Apostolic?

It is said that coming down the main walk from the Washington capitol towards Pennsylvania Avenue, there was once a group of steps very confusing to the average pedestrian of the late 1800s. Watching the crowds, a man saw people continually stumbling on these steps, while they did not do so on others.

Mr. Frederick Olmstead, one of the capitol's architects, was called to look into the matter, and he was amazed to see how many people stumbled while walking up those steps. "I cannot account for it," he said. "I spent weeks arranging those steps. I had wooden models of them put down at my own place, and I walked over them day after day until I felt sure they were perfect."

"Isn't one of your legs shorter than the other, Mr. Olmstead?" someone asked. He was dumbfounded when it flashed over him that, owing to the inequality of his own limbs; he had made steps for the capitol unsuited for any except people who had the same defect.[iv]

We really can't judge ourselves and our own work, because we won't be objective. Our defects get in the way, and we'll prefer the self that feels most comfortable. It's the same with the church. We can't just have church the way it feels best for . . . me. We need to know what a church ought to be — its characteristics determined by the Lord of the Church — and then strive to conform it to His will.

What Is the House Really Like?

In this chapter, we'll see that churches, if they are to be true apostolic houses, must have certain basic traits or common denominators. I've listed virtually all of these in diagrams: *(See Appendices 3–10 on pages 145–155.)*

Key Characteristics of an Apostolic House

It is a house of . . .

◆ vision and strategy; government, rank, and order;

◆ prophetic expression, sound preaching and teaching, allowing for exploration that moves into the realm of revelation;

◆ stable families, where family-centered values are taught and practiced;

◆ prayer, a house filled with intercessors, with much teaching about the purposes of prayer;

◆ prosperity and blessing, where there are signs of prosperity by what is taught;

◆ bold faith, where faith takes preeminence, and faith goes into new territory and new ground;

◆ healing, miracles, deliverance, missions, praise and worship.

♦ social care, where the needs of people are being met in practical ways;

♦ gifts of the Spirit and the Spiritual gifts;

♦ leadership training, discipleship, mentoring, and developing children and youth for the future;

♦ cell ministries or small groups;

♦ business entities, where entrepreneurs provide financially;

♦ technology, where technological pursuits are insisted upon. (How can a church trying to reach twenty-first-century people remain in the 1950s?)

Now I'd like to pick out several of these charted qualities to explore in greater depth. They are crucial, so I'll try to build a case around each of them.

It must be a house of vision.

You cannot have an apostolic house without vision. The Scripture is clear: *"Where there is no vision, the people perish"* (Proverbs 29:18). But what is vision? Here is one definition:

Vision: the capacity to create a compelling picture of the desired state of affairs that inspires people to respond; that which is desirable, which could be, should be; that which is attainable. A godly vision is right for the times, right for the church, and right for the people. A godly vision promotes faith rather than fear. A godly vision motivates people to action. A godly vision requires risk-taking. A godly vision glorifies God, not people.[v]

God is structuring a new vision mandate for the twenty-first-century church — what is desirable, attain-able, and brings glory to His name. This vision must be multi-generational, spanning several generations. If we're not going to build ministries to last at least a hundred years, then we're wasting our time because our great-grandchildren must be able to enjoy what we have started.

Thus our visionary apostles must be constantly structuring a tomorrow. If a church ever loses its tomorrow, and that tomorrow becomes today, then that church dies today.

About 350 years ago, a shipload of travelers landed on the northeast coast of America. The first year they established a town site. The next year they elected a town government. The third year the town government planned to build a road five miles westward into the wilderness.

In the fourth year the people tried to impeach their town government because they thought it was a waste of public funds to build a road five miles westward into a wilderness. Who needed to go there anyway?

Here were people who had the vision to see three thousand miles across an ocean and overcome great hardships to get there. But in just a few years they were not able to see even five miles out of town. They had lost their pioneering vision. With a clear vision of what we can become in Christ, no ocean of difficulty is too great. Without it, we rarely move beyond our current boundaries.vi

It must be a house of government and rank.

Government and rank are critically important, because if a church doesn't function governmentally, the devil will rule and reign instead! All cities therefore need apostolic houses that have government, rank, and order.

Where the order of God is maintained, leaders at least have access to rank. In other words, even if ranked men and women are not in a particular house, it's leadership can have access to that rank through making a phone call, sending a fax or an email, and have an apostolic leader come to their ministry. Government and rank are in their "down-line," so to speak. Apostolic leaders of rank can then come in and deal with a demonic problem.

For example, if there is a tremendous spiritual attack on a church, and we know that it's an attack of witchcraft, if we don't have the rank and order in the house to deal with this, we'd better have somebody available down-line. Successful apostolic houses have access to those with the authority to deal with such things.

It must be a house of prophetic expression.

The prophetic word actually molds and shapes the church, because the prophetic ministry does a number of things:

♦ It releases the destiny of God in a place;

♦ It tells us what's coming in our immediate future and builds our faith to get it;

♦ It releases the gifts of men and women to meet practical and spiritual needs.

The prophetic gift is so important because it shapes us into the image of Christ and brings us into the future of all that Christ wants us to be. So an apostolic house must have the prophetic in powerful doses. Yet it always needs to submit to what God is saying in visions and dreams, to what God is saying in prayer, to what God is saying in sound preaching and teaching.

The prophetic is so much more than just preaching and teaching that brings an emotional high. The prophetic ministry changes people's lives so they receive a strategy, a new basis for successful living. In our own ministry we call such forms of teaching "power nuggets" or "success power talks." We'll invite people to come to us and offer a power talk on various disciplines such as pursuing excellence, or developing a financial strategy, nurturing healthy family relation-ships, or coping with healthcare needs. All of these nuggets teach, reshape, and transform the minds of people open to God's prophetic Word.

It must be a house of strong families.

A woman was at home doing some cleaning when the telephone rang. In going to answer it, she tripped on a rug and, grabbing for something to hold onto, seized the telephone table. It fell over with a crash, jarring the receiver off the hook. As it fell, it hit the family dog, who leaped up, howling and barking. The woman's three-year-old son, startled by this noise, broke into loud screams. The woman mumbled some colorful words. She finally managed to pick up the receiver and lift it to her ear — just in time to hear her husband's voice on the other end, saying to someone near him: "Nobody has said hello yet, but I'm positive I have the right number."[vii]

In so many ways, just like this, the devil is attacking families. And our stress and exhaustion with daily life can quickly become a spiritual problem. If we have weak families — or no solid families in the house — then the fabric of the future has been eroded and destroyed.

What, then, is a strong family? I came across a national survey of strong families conducted by the Human Development and Family Department at the University of Nebraska (Lincoln), a profile of a strong family:

Appreciation. *"Family members gave one another compliments and sincere demonstrations of approval. They tried to make the others feel appreciated and good about themselves."*

Ability to Deal with Crises in a Positive Manner. *"They were willing to take a bad situation, see something positive in it, and focus on that."*

Time Together. *"In all areas of their lives — meals, work, recreation — they structured their schedules to spend time together."*

High Degree of Commitment. *"Families promoted each person's happiness and welfare, invested time and energy in each other, and made family their number-one priority."*

Good Communication Patterns. *"These families spent time talking with each other. They also listened well, which shows respect."*

High Degree of Religious Orientation. *"Not all belonged to an organized church, but they considered themselves highly religious."*[viii]

Rudyard Kipling once wrote about families, *"All of us are we, and everyone else is they."* A family shares things like dreams, hopes, possessions, memories, smiles, frowns, and gladness. A family is a clan held together with the glue of love and the cement of mutual respect. A family is shelter from the storm, a friendly port when the waves of life become too wild. No person is ever alone when he's a member of a family.

Perhaps the best way to begin strengthening our families is to determine to be sacrificially kind to one another, as much as possible. Simply put, men: An exhaustive study shows that no woman has ever shot her husband while he was doing the dishes.

There's Variety Here!

We've looked at key qualities of the successful apostolic house. Now it's time to recognize that they come in various flavors or types. I'm speaking of differing structures, strategies, and ministry emphases. For example, an apostolic house may have an apostolic emphasis. Our church, New Life Covenant Church, is that kind of a house. But an apostolic house may have a prophetic structure and emphasis. Or it may have an evangelistic structure and emphasis. Furthermore, it may have a pastoral structure or a teaching structure. Let me explain — comparing and contrasting — by using the two most common emphases: the apostolic and the prophetic.

The house may have an APOSTOLIC structure and strategy.

This is a ministry led by a team of apostles, people who, when they see something apparently good happening in the world . . . they don't immediately seek to emulate it. For example, if there's a move of God such as there was in Toronto or in Pensacola, or a breakout of the Holy Spirit in Saskatchewan, they won't be unduly enthusiastic about implementing what they're seeing. If there's an outbreak of laughter in a certain place, an apostolic house with an apostolic structure is not going to try to implement that manifestation in their house.

Instead, they may send representatives to document everything about that particular move of God. They'll ask: Is this an authentic move of God? Can the Word of God substantiate it with credibility? Is it authenticated by reliable, independent, prophetic and apostolic voices in the body of Christ who aren't directly related to this move of God? Can they say unequivocally that this is a release of God that is not of the flesh, that is not demonic, that is not a strategy of the enemy?

Once these things have been determined, then these leaders will search for the scriptural support or basis. If they find that support, then they may well decide to seek and implement that move of God in a structured way among them — not to change the church or its direction or structure, but to allow that phenomenon to be introduced as a benefit for the people.

Our own ministry is an apostolic house with an apostolic emphasis. It means that we are well structured apostolically. Most of what we do is Word-based, in terms of authenticating certain moves of God. That's why you can come to New Life Covenant Church and you will not see banners. You will not have prophetic dances in every service because we are an apostolic house with an apostolic emphasis. We make room for the prophetic, so once in a while we get someone to do a prophetic dance, or we'll hang a few banners. But that's not our emphasis.

Our emphasis is more on structure, strategy, vision, and systems. We are leader-oriented. We impart skill to leaders, many times in a prophetic way. We make room for a move of the Holy Spirit, in that we're not going to demand that we always sing two songs, have preaching, and then close the service. If the Holy Spirit is moving during the songs, we'll sing all day. But then, when we come back to the next service, we're going to explain scripturally what happened.

Because we have an apostolic emphasis, we don't allow outbursts and manifestations without first proving them and explaining those kinds of things. So if somebody bursts out in tongues at the wrong time, and speaks in a prayer language and then tries to give an interpretation, we will correct that person and teach him or her to do it the right way, because we are an apostolic house with an apostolic emphasis.

We are not so rigid that we try to stop God from moving! But we are not so loose that we allow anything to happen any time it wants to happen. Nobody can run to the front and grab a microphone and start prophesying; they'll be stopped right there and asked, "What's up with you?" Because we are an apostolic house with an apostolic emphasis.

The house may have a PROPHETIC structure and strategy.

When you have an apostolic house with a prophetic structure, an apostle leads the house, but everything is prophetic. For example, the curtains in that place will actually mean something. They'll have purple curtains that speak of royalty, or blue curtains that speak of passion, or red curtains that speak of Christ's blood.

If they've got a vase of roses, they'll have twelve roses, because twelve means government; they won't have eleven, because eleven doesn't mean anything. All of their banners will be metaphoric, and in every service there will be prophesies. In fact, the services will be designed around the prophetic anointing.

My brother's church is this way, where almost everything they do is prophetic. It's the kind of house where, if it's the tenth day of the tenth month, then ten is a significant number.

I don't live my life that way. There are times when I will mention things like that, because I am an apostolic house with an apostolic emphasis and we draw from the prophetic. But I don't live my life that way. I don't count the row here and say, "My, this row has eleven chairs, bring in one more to make it twelve." I don't care if there's one chair; it doesn't mean anything to me. Of course, if God speaks to me and says, "Set up twelve chairs," then we'll do it. But we're not going to do everything prophetically.

I want you to understand that houses with specific areas of emphasis are not incorrect in their structure. All apostolic houses must accept other kinds of houses. The problems come when some ministries say of others: "Oh, they're not prophetic. They don't have a deliverance ministry, and they don't pray all night. They don't have 24-hour prayer, so they're doing it all wrong!"

That's not the right stance to take; it can even be dangerous. There were twelve apostles, and each of them had a different kind of structure and ministry.

4

UNDERSTANDING GOVERNMENTAL RULE

In his book *OPERATION WORLD* one of my fellow Zimbabweans, Pat Johnson, claims that some 700 million people received the baptism of the Holy Spirit during the twentieth century. Yet in spite of this wonderful news — and all the blessings it has brought into human lives — God's people still do not have dominion upon the earth. Satan is still in control here; in large measure he rules . . .

. . . the money,

. . . the political arenas,

. . . the economic forces,

. . . the entertainment world,

. . . the environment,

. . . the media and air waves,

. . . the educational institutions,

. . . the religious power-players.

I'm sure you could expand this list. After all, is there any sphere in which he is not exerting a vast influence for evil? This breaks my heart. It is why I write — and why the message of this chapter must go forth.

We need not despair, however. God is restoring authority to His people on earth. Not just the kind of authority in which a man may cast out a devil. No, it's the ruling authority that comes packaged with Christ's government among us. And we know this about our Lord Jesus Christ: *"The government shall be upon his shoulder: and . . . of the increase of his government and peace there shall be no end"* (Isaiah 9:6-7). The new church order is our rule and reign with Christ in heavenly places.

Sadly, we have hardly known this aspect of our faith. We have not seen Christ's powerful influence extended across the globe under a unity of leadership. Our "ministry generals" have failed, have continued in their own camps, raising their own finances, and building their own kingdoms. They have not used their anointing to address global issues — or even national ones.

I say this respectfully, but God has blessed them with millions and millions of dollars to finance their office as generals in the body of Christ, and they've confined that ministry. It remains within a city headquarters or home office, or some other center of operation. They haven't gone outside to address the wide-ranging rule of demonic spirits.

This generation is quickly coming to an end.

A new generation of generals is rising. They are realizing: "God hasn't called me just to be another little church somewhere in town." God is raising them up to rule and reign in continents. Again, they are recognizing: "The kind of anointing God is bringing here isn't just for me to pray for people to get saved in my silly little town." They see that it takes a group of people with an anointing that can master the Spirit world and go wherever on the globe this authority desperately needs releasing.

It's not just about starting a church and preaching well in a robe, and sweating, and doing a dance step for an hour or two. It's about taking authority in the heavenlies. That can only happen when we are willing to establish government.

The Scripture says of David, that when he came to power as the king, God gave him peace from all his enemies *(see 2 Samuel 7)*. The reason: David brought order and government.

How did he do it? How does governmental rule come into being? The rest of this chapter will dig into these questions. It is David's story of accomplishing four prophetic deeds that eventually brings full governmental rule to God's people.

He Kills the Killer

David begins as a shepherd, looking after a few sheep spread out across a Judean mountainside. He is not the obvious choice for greatness, to become the ruler of the nation. After all, he is the youngest of seven sons and "thrown in the back" to look after somebody else's sheep. The others hardly care that he'll be facing lions and bears out there! (Which, incidentally, he takes care of in his "private time." because private quiet time allows us to have public performance. It is in those moments of having to slay the attacking beasts that God opens the future to us.) He slays the animals, but God has sent him to do much more — to slay a killer giant, a nine-foot tall behemoth who would destroy the nation.

His Selection of Weapons Is Key.

In Judea, stones abound. But David did not take stones from anywhere on the hillside. Instead, he went to the river to find five small pebbles. Why? Because the river had running water; those stones had been tempered by seasonal flushings of water, seasonal revelations, seasonal outpourings. We think of "the washing of the water by the Word" and therefore understand: David had to select giant stones — or revelatory words, or anointings — that had been subjected to seasonal flows.

He takes up five stones (not six; five, referring to the apostolic mantle and mandate: apostle, prophet, evangelist, pastor, and teacher) but puts only one stone in his slingshot. He swings and hits the giant in the forehead, right where the mark of the beast would be, where Satan would put his number, the 666 on those he owns. David hits giant Goliath square on the mark, and brings down Satanic government with the ministry of an apostle. David then stands on the dead giant's chest and takes off his head with the man's own sword. David's measure of rule is thus extended.

I believe God has led you to the river, as well. It's pointless standing at the river and saying, "By the rivers of Babylon, we stood there and wept when we remembered the good old days of Zion." We're not standing at this river to weep. We're standing like a tree planted by the rivers of water . . . that shall not be moved. But we are also very careful in our selection of stones; we are taking out specific weapons to rule and reign with Christ.

As the church takes up this reign, it will transform all who come to it. When people start walking through church doors depleted, bankrupt, sick, tired, messed up, dysfunctional; they're going to walk into a place where they feel the authority of the Kingdom. It will go deeper than anointing, because anointed people can be in the choir, sing under anointing, and still go out and sleep around. Some folks have the anointing and also beat their wives. Some still lie and cheat. But when we're dealing with authority, it's a different matter. When people see the authority of the house, they remember Ananias and Sapphira, and they do not walk the lifestyle of a lie.

He Carts the Container.

Container? I'm speaking of the ark of the covenant, Israel's precious, gold-lidded box that contained three holy things: Aaron's rod that budded, a golden pot of manna, and the tablets of the ten commandments. Aaron's rod stands for the discernment the people of Israel needed in order to choose the tribe of Levi for the priesthood *(see Numbers 17:2-11)*; the pot of manna stands for the knowledge the people needed to follow God's instructions about how and when to eat in the desert (see Exod. 16); the ten commandments stand for the wisdom the people needed to know what was right and wrong behavior as they sought to live for God *(see Exodus 20:1-17)*.

Recall that once a year, on the Day of Atonement, Aaron the priest would sprinkle blood on the pure-gold covering over the Ark of the Covenant, known as the mercy seat. There God's glory would come, and it was there on that mercy seat, which represented God's government, that the state of perfection would be released. All the enemies of Israel — sickness, disease, poverty, demonic spirits, hostile kings and kingdoms — all would be subdued under the power of God. That Day of Atonement was called the state of perfection, when that which was perfect had come. That which was in part, which was in proxy, was done away.

So when the Ark of the Covenant was given to the children of Israel, they took it everywhere with them. The priests carried it upon their shoulders as the nation marched into battle with God's government. Thus, everywhere God's government came, the enemies had to fall, whether Goliath and the Philistines, or the sons of Anoch or the Perizzites, or the Hittites. All had to fall.

But there came a day when the Philistines captured the ark (because of the sin of Phineas, who took the ark into battle without divine authorization). These enemies tried to bring the Philistine system upon the Ark of the Covenant by putting it in the camp of their god, Dagon (his name means "little fish"; they were people of the sea and worshiped a fish-god). Look what happened . . .

> *When the Philistines took the ark of God, they brought it into the house of Dagon, and set it by Dagon. And when they of Ashdod arose early on the morrow, behold, Dagon was fallen upon his face to the earth before the ark of the LORD. And they took Dagon, and set him in his place again.*

> *And when they arose early on the morrow morning, behold, Dagon was fallen upon his face to the ground before the ark of the LORD; and the head of Dagon and both the palms of his hands were cut off upon the threshold; only the stump of Dagon was left to him.*

> *Therefore neither the priests of Dagon, nor any that come into Dagon's house, tread on the threshold of Dagon in Ashdod unto this day.*
>
> —1 Samuel 5:2-5

Please take a moment to read the entire story found in 1 Samuel 5 and 6. But suffice it to say here that the government of the Philistines could not make subservient the government of God. The ark caused them lots of problems! So, when the Philistines repented of taking the ark, they sent it back to Israel with two milk cows that had just given birth.

They were testing to see whether this ark was more powerful than the laws of nature. I grew up on a farm, and my grandfather had cattle. When it's time for the little calves to start sucking, nature demands that the mother cow find her calf. But when the ark was on its way toward Israel, those cows — even though they were full with milk to give — would not turn away from a mission God had set for them. The Bible says they marched all the way to Beth-shemesh.

A man named Joshua was in the field reaping corn and wheat when the ark stood right there in the middle of this Joshua's field.

The first thing this man did — he wasn't even a priest, but he recognized the anointing of God — was to slay those milk cows. He also took the cows carrying the ark, made a fire, and sacrificed them. He wasn't authorized to be a priest, but there are times when we walk under God's government, and God makes unusual provisions for us.

Eventually David, who had been made king *(see the story in 2 Samuel chapters 4–7)*, goes to fetch this ark. His first attempt failed when Uzzah touched the ark and died. (Uzzah was trying to steady it but was killed.) In touching the ark, it was not the presence of God that he touched; it was the government of God that he touched. For the Bible tells us, *"In [God's] presence, there is fullness of joy."* So when he touched the ark, the touching was actually the man literally touching God's government. No one can touch God's government and get away with it. Ask Lucifer. He was expelled with lightning when he did it.

Yet David feared at seeing the awesome power of God. Instead of moving on toward the city of David, he carted the ark off to the side of the road and into to Obed-edom's house. When the ark came into Obed-edom's house, everything in Obed-edom's measure of rule, where the government was, God blessed. Everything in Obed-edom's possession was blessed because God's government had extended his measure of rule.

He Brings the Blessing . . . Home

David saw the blessing God's government brought and said, in effect, "Obed-edom can't get blessed alone! We've got to bring this ark home" *(2 Samuel 6:12)*. So what did David do? He didn't call a board meeting, he didn't have any elder meetings, nor did he gather all the generals together.

So David went and brought up the ark of God from the house of Obed-edom into the city of David with gladness.

And it was so, that when they that bare the ark of the LORD had gone six paces, he sacrificed oxen and fatlings.

And David danced before the LORD with all his might; and David was girded with a linen ephod.

So David and all the house of Israel brought up the ark of the LORD with shouting, and with the sound of the trumpet...

And as soon as David had made an end of offering burnt offerings and peace offerings, he blessed the people in the name of the LORD of hosts.

And he dealt among all the people, even among the whole multitude of Israel, as well to the women as men, to every one a cake of bread, and a good piece of flesh, and a flagon of wine. So all the people departed every one to his house.

—2 Samuel 6:12-15, 18-19

He retrieved the ark and then he exulted in praise. He danced six steps, and then offered a sacrifice. He gave pieces of meat to all those participating; they gave wine, gave bread and anointed with oil, all around the place and then they danced six steps again.

How shall we understand all these things? We could say that we're at the end of the sixth day (the 6000th year from the creation of Adam). At the end of the sixth day, the government is coming home! We've had Obed-edom in various organizations, in various churches, where their measure of rule was blessed. But now, in the sixth day — in six steps — we sacrifice, we rejoice and we dance. They were giving out flagons of wine and healthy portions of meat and bread; right there, every six steps. The richest blessing of the entire kingdom is coming at the end of the sixth step, the sixth day. The government of God is coming home. *[FOR MORE DETAILED EXPLANATION SEE REFERENCES LISTED IN THE AUTHOR'S NOTE AT THE BEGINNING OF THE BOOK.]*

Where is the ark at this moment as they're moving towards the Jebusite camp or Zion? It's on the shoulders of the priests. On the shoulders of apostolic houses, on the shoulders of apostolic priesthood, a royal priest-hood moving to a place so the measure of rule can be extended.

Isaiah 11 says there's a day coming when a rod springs out of the root of Jesse, and a branch. He refers to Christ and the church. The branch is coming out of the rod, Christ and His church. In Isaiah 11:2, the Bible says, *"And the spirit of the LORD shall rest upon him."* (This means male and female. In Genesis 5:1-2, God made Adam and Eve, and he called *their* name *Adam,* meaning *one flesh.*)

We are about to walk in the fullness of the glory of Jesus Christ. He is upgrading the standard of anointing in the body. The bride of Christ is going to be the most anointed being the earth has ever known. It's going to be the answer to the problems, sicknesses, diseases and economic and politic instabilities all over the world. The answers are coming through the church, because of intercessory prayer, and because of fivefold ministry being restored. But the last thing is the government of God coming back to its rightful place — as it was with David: the blessing is brought home.

He Removes the Robes

David accomplishes a fourth prophetic deed. He takes off his fine kingly "threads."

> *And Michal the daughter of Saul came out to meet David, and said, How glorious was the king of Israel today, who uncovered himself today in the eyes of the handmaids of his servants, as one of the vain fellows shamelessly uncovereth himself!*
>
> —2 Samuel 6:20

Saul's daughter didn't like David's wild exuberance in his praise. She didn't like watching him lose himself in God's blessing. But David worshiped from the heart.

And maybe it is a bit humorous. Maybe he finds a little junior priest somewhere and says, "How would you like to be a king for a day?" I can just see David putting a heavy crown on the head of this junior priest, who's sitting around the corner hiding behind a bush. He puts on this man the kingly purple and blue and scarlet robes. The man is ruling, just for a single day.

A day with the Lord is as a thousand years and a thousand years as one day. Here's this priest scared to death of what's happening to him, but here's David the king rejoicing as a priest.

For the past two thousand years we have been priests and not kings. Jesus has been king and not priest. The role is about to reverse — the first shall be last and the last shall be first. We are now going to see the priestly ministry of Jesus Christ and the kingly ministry of the body of Christ come into perspective, a joining of power and strength. Where the two are joined together, what God has joined together, let no man put asunder. We are about to witness an outpouring of God's power, grace, and mercy — a day in which all of the subduers are coming right under our foot.

The Bible says that when David placed the ark on Zion, it didn't go back to Shiloh because Shiloh had served its time a hundred years prior to that. It was now on Zion. The difference being: it was now open for everybody to see. The glory of God was shining through there, and everybody who came could see it. They worshiped around it.

In all the days of David and Solomon, they had peace. David faced a few quickly subdued uprisings because of his sin. But in Solomon's day, all the days of his life, not one enemy raised his hand, because the government was in its rightful place.

What Power!

Do we realize the power of governmental rule under God's authority? Think about it. I leave you to contem-plate the words of writer Annie Dillard: *"Does anyone have the foggiest idea of what sort of power we so blithely invoke? Or, as I suspect, does no one believe a word of it? The churches are children playing on the floor with their chemistry sets, mixing up a batch of TNT to kill a Sunday morning. It is madness to wear ladies' straw hats and velvet hats to church; we should all be wearing crash helmets. Ushers should issue life preservers and signal flares; they should lash us to our pews.* [ix]

5

Put Deliverance on the Menu!

When God makes you an apostolic house, you need to include certain things on your menu. That is, God creates a power in ministry, and that ministry will have certain traits. Furthermore, when people order what's on the menu, they're supposed to get it.

One of the often-missing items is deliverance. Jesus said:

> The Spirit of the Lord is upon me, because he hath anointed me to preach the gospel to the poor; he hath sent me to heal the brokenhearted, to **preach deliverance** to the captives . . .   —Luke 4:18

We are to take up the preaching Jesus was doing before He ascended to heaven. We are his mouthpiece until He returns. Therefore we, too, need to preach deliverance to the captives. It's not enough that we proclaim a great Gospel, and people come to give their hearts to the Lord. People only come to church for a few hours a week and thus what they do with the rest of their week is very important. The preaching of deliverance is crucial for them.

I realize, though, that folks in affluent societies may not want to face such things. It is certainly easier to major on the pleasant aspects of Jesus — His promises of peace and rest and eternal life. Or we might prefer a message of positive thinking to spiritual warfare, a "think and grow rich" seminar over a confrontation with evil. Yet while such messages might increase our sense of comfort in the world, they do not change the world.

And world changing is our mission, isn't it?

As much as we may wish to avoid it, Jesus did speak of evil spirits, of demons, of the devil himself. He stood up to them and rebuked them. When the lake storm arose, for instance, and Jesus slept in the boat, his disciples cried out to him: "Don't you care that we're going to die?" Awaking, Jesus did not take a barometric pressure reading. He did not give a weather forecast or suggest ways to secure the boat. No, he rebuked an evil force — something that had no choice but to obey.

If you are still tentative about such things, then allow me to speak about Africa for a moment. There I witness the workings of evil in full Technicolor, with my own eyes, day in and day out. No one living there could ever deny that myriad demonic spirits bind Africa. One of the reasons is the devil has legal tender among so many of the people. He has legal rights to their land and their families. Why? Because their ancestors, of the past — or their ancestor-worship religions of the present — have invited him to take over.

It makes no difference that the invitation is subtler here in America. Satan still responds, and we must break the legal right in both places — in all places! In the West, he often gains legal rights through such things as new-age worship, occult practices, astrology, horoscopes, or sexual perversion.

In so many churches, we're naïve because we've felt that, having repented, having received the Holy Spirit, we are now exempt from enemy attack. No, you and I are not exempt (a quick review of

Ephesians 6:11-18 should set us straight on this point). You will be visited from time to time.

But how can you tell whether you have demonic ties, or whether a demonic spirit is seeking a legal hold in your life? There are some major "inlets" such forces might use to get through to us: through personal sin, through soul ties, through unforgiveness, and through bloodlines.

Put Away Personal Sin!

Personal sin gives the demonic powers legal rights. There's nothing mysterious about this, either. Think about all the people who are constantly angry, mad about everything, screaming at traffic, hollering at their children, flying off the handle at any slight provocation. Can we really blame such over-the-top reactions on normal impatience or irritability? I don't think so. We know that such irrational raging is sin. We also know that sinful anger gives demonic spirits an inroad to the soul.

I have my own experience with this. When I am deathly tired — especially when I'm home, and the children are making lots of noise — I can let my anger fly. About three years ago I began to think it through:

Is this strengthening my family life?

Is it endearing to my wife?

Is it growing me into a more Christ-like man of God?

I began to pray and ask God to cleanse me and forgive me from apparent anger in my life. But I also recognized that it wasn't just irritation because I was tired; it was actually a demonic spirit. I had to ask God to bring deliverance into my life. None of us, under any circumstance, can afford to tolerate ongoing personal sin.

Consider sexual sin as another example. I was preaching in a country a few years ago and merely mentioned sexual sin. I immediately felt a spirit of opposition rising up and challenging my words. I turned around and said, "In this choir, there are sexually active young people; this ought not to be." Eight of those choir members came to me after the service and repented.

But many in the church, offended at my direct manner of preaching, requested that I never come back. I followed the progress of that church, though. A few months later, a girl in the choir announced that she was pregnant by the choir director. The pastor said to the man, "You will no longer be leading the choir, and you will no longer be ministering here in any other way."

What happened then? Half of the choir members said to the pastor, "If you make him step down, then we are all out of here, because most of us are sexually active anyway."

This situation broke a strong, thriving church in that country. The congregation is now a shell of what it could have been. But suppose they had listened to the word of an apostolic authority that night? Suppose they had repented of personal sin? They could have seen young couples coming to the altar asking forgiveness; instead, they gave the devil a legal right to them.

There is no clearer way to say it: Personal sin gives the devil property rights on you. And the Bible just as clearly says: *"Give no place to the devil"* (Ephesians 4:27). In this text, the original Greek word for "place" is *topos*, the same word from which we get "topography" — the study of the land. So give the devil no land, no property in your life. Give him no ground, no room, no reason, no occasion. Just don't give way!

We will fall and fail, of course. So let us walk in a constant state of repentance, which is one of the greatest gifts God has given mankind. Giving place to the devil means making friends with your sins. The call from God is just the opposite. It is a call to confront the truth of your daily weakness and to move ahead in His grace:

> *If we say that we have no sin, we deceive ourselves, and the truth is not in us. If we confess our sins, he is faithful and*

just to forgive us our sins, and to cleanse us from all unrighteousness. —1 John 1:8-9

Sever the Soul Ties

The devil gets a legal hold, not only through personal sin but also through ungodly relationships with persons or things. What do I mean? The apostle Paul put it this way:

What fellowship hath righteousness with unrighteousness? And what communion hath light with darkness? And what concord hath Christ with Belial? Or what part hath he that believeth with an infidel? And what agreement hath the temple of God with idols? For ye are the temple of the living God; as God hath said, I will dwell in them, and walk in them; and I will be their God, and they shall be my people.

Wherefore come out from among them, and be ye separate, saith the Lord, and touch not the unclean thing; and I will receive you, and will be a Father unto you, and ye shall be my sons and daughters, saith the Lord Almighty.

Having therefore these promises, dearly beloved, let us cleanse ourselves from all filthiness of the flesh and spirit, perfecting holiness in the fear of God.

—2 Corinthians 6:14b-7:1

A soul tie occurs when your soul — your being — is joined legally to that of another person or system. Typically ties are established through sexual union. In such cases, all of the entities — demonic spirits, curses, sins — flow into a person, just like that. It's like a spiritual AIDS, in which, through soul-bonding contact, you receive the other's disease.

When a husband goes on a business trip and has a one-night stand with a woman he doesn't know anything about, all of that woman's demonic curses, for generations gone by, come onto this man. Then he comes home. And he has sexual intercourse with his wife. That woman's uncleanness comes onto his wife. Then when the wife is breast-feeding; all of the stuff from that woman now goes onto the children. The years go by. Then the son turns sixteen, and the parents wonder what happened to this boy. He was showing some spark, going to be a great kid. But now he's gone wild. Did the husband consider his destructive soul tie?

Soul ties are destroying us today, because so many people now consider it normal to have multiple sex partners in a lifetime. ChiChi and I prayed for a young lady, let's call her Jane, as she lay dying in St. Anne's Hospital in Harare. She had been baptized, had received the Holy Ghost, but denied having AIDS. However, a week before she died, she asked for us and made this confession: "Pastor, in the past two years, knowing full well I was HIV-positive, I slept with fifty different men."

Jane could not get healing. It wasn't because God wasn't able to heal, nor was it because we had no authority and anointing to heal. But the devil had so many legal holds in that lady. We just didn't have the knowledge of how to bring true deliverance to Jane. In fact, her body was so weak that we couldn't do it.

Think about how often Jesus would first cast out a spirit before healing a person. Many times, when we're praying for people to be healed we expect them to immediately step out of their wheelchairs or drop their crutches. They can't, there's a soul tie needing to be broken first.

It's not just a person-to-person bond. Many people have soul ties with alcohol, cigarettes, drugs, porno-graphy, or the occult. They need deliverance, because no one can have spiritual intercourse with a spirit and think they're going to remain unharmed. Satan will claim what has been offered to him.

Will you seek the power of deliverance in your life? Will you put it on the menu in your apostolic house? We can't afford to ignore the inroads of evil while we preach the goodness of God.

Undo Unforgiveness

Unforgiveness gives the demonic tremendous power. We knew a wonderful young lady in our church whose husband was once very strong in the congregation. But he held bitterness inside; he hated his father.

It wasn't without reason. When this man was a child, his father had walked out and moved in with the lady next door. He saw it break his mother and throw the whole family into poverty. He just couldn't forgive his dad.

He came to Christ and married one of our sweetest girls. One day they went to a shopping center and, just as they were parking, he saw his father. His wife was still getting out of the car when he slammed the car into reverse, throwing his wife to the pavement. He started cursing and yelling, "Get in the car!"

He was a deacon in the church. So his wife and everybody else were amazed and wondered what was going on. But just the sight of his father brought out an unearthly vehemence in this man, replete with obscene language never heard in a deacon's meeting!

He continued his seething rage at his father, and the years have gone by. I am sad to report that the way his father treated his mother is exactly the way this man now treats his own wife. The devil has a legal hold on this man, through the spirit of unforgiveness. The former deacon won't come to church. He's bitter, spiteful, having let into his life that which seeks his destruction.

Why should we hinder the blessings of each new day with unforgiveness? If you are unforgiving in any way — whether you've been hurt by a fellow church member, a spouse, a relative, a boss, or a neighbor — realize that you are opening yourself to demonic influence. You must forgive, for the consequences of holding onto your hurt are horrific:

> *If ye forgive not men their trespasses, neither will your Father forgive your trespasses.* —Matthew 6:15

If a church somewhere has hurt you, and bruised you, let forgiveness flow into your heart. If you've been abused by a parent, oppressed by a government, vio-lated by a preacher . . . invite the peace and presence of the One who turned His cheek and willingly went the extra mile. It can only bring healing to your soul. Even if this message is making you angry right now, begin to release your hold on vengeance. That is God's business alone.

The reason Nelson Mandela is a giant among men is that he willingly sat in prison for twenty-eight years. He was abused, constantly beaten, treated with unrelenting malice. Yet to his captors, every night, no matter how they treated him, he would say: "Goodnight, sir." They couldn't understand how this man could be so kind. When he was finally sworn into office as president of South Africa, he issued a decree of forgiveness and reconciliation — even though people in his family had been brutally and unjustly killed.

Why forgive? Because if you don't, you give the devil a *topos* — a ground, a place, a little room inside you. It doesn't mean we don't hold wrongdoers responsible or accountable for their actions. It does mean that we don't hold them in our hatred. If God continues to love them, so can we.

Lewis B. Smedes, in his book FORGIVE AND FORGET[x] offers three wonderful statements for us to meditate upon as I close out this section:

♦ As we forgive people, we gradually come to see the deeper truth about them, a truth our hate blinds us to, a truth we can see only when we separate them from what they did to us. When we heal our memories we are not playing games, we are not making believe. We see the truth again. For the truth about those who hurt us is that they are weak, needy, and fallible human beings. They were people before they hurt us and they are people after they hurt us.

♦ Forgiving is tough. Excusing is easy. What a mistake it is to confuse forgiving with being mush, soft, gutless, and oh, so understanding. Before we forgive, we stiffen our spine and we hold a person accountable. And only then, with tough-minded judgment, can we do the outrageously impossible thing: we can forgive.

♦ Forgiveness: You know it has started when you begin to wish that person well.

Beware the Bloodlines

Ancestral curses flow through bloodlines. Churches must deal with this.

Here is my recommendation. Begin to deal with people on this level immediately after they've received Christ. Once they have prayed what is commonly called "The Sinner's Prayer," invite them to make a verbal declaration before the church: "I accept Jesus Christ to be the head of my new government. I renounce the past."

Once that has happened, they can then willingly go into the back somewhere where a leader, elder, or pastor, can begin to give instruction and explore this individual's past. Maybe he or she was involved with the occult, a practice passed down from the family bloodlines. Maybe this woman has been abused, maybe this man has been involved in homosexuality, and maybe this person has been into drugs.

They're fighting for their lives!

You see, so many seekers coming into our churches know nothing of theology. They have little concern for hermeneutics, homiletics, or eschatology. They don't care about epistemological terminology. All they know is, "I want . . . desire . . . need . . ." So they come seeking. Then you give them an altar call and you botch it up because they have to stand there and mumble.

Take them back and ask, "What do you need?" Maybe they say, "My parents were always on drugs, and I need to get free of that curse." You'll find a soul tie there. You'll find a need for deliverance from demonic powers. (We have underestimated the power of drugs, which will hold whole family bloodlines for decades.)

We baptize people who are not ready to be baptized, just so we can produce a pleasing statistic. Baptism is the sign of a covenant. But how can someone profess a sign of a covenant if they don't have a clue what covenant is? Yet we baptize, and six months later our convert is back in the world.

But if we show them that this is the covenant, this is the power of the covenant, and these are the rights of your covenant — and we're going to break every hold the devil has on your life by doing this — then we bring them deliverance. Their profession of Christ takes hold, and they begin living for him.

I'm simply saying: When people come forward, don't give them terminology, give them Jesus. And don't leave them with a surface acceptance of their Savior. Open up the depths so Christ can flow down deep and make His home there. Cast out the devils to make room for the Spirit!

If you will pay close attention to the potential inroads of evil, you'll see families getting healed, children growing up right, people's attitudes being sorted out, as demonic spirits are removed, and strongholds are broken down. Your house is going to be an apostolic house. You'll offer a full menu that brings the Kingdom to bear in full measure.

6

BECOMING A HOUSE OF PRAYER

I was preaching on one of my "Meet the People" tours in Africa. In one area, we have ten churches, so I brought all the preachers together late one Friday afternoon. After addressing these leaders, I separated myself to prepare for a ten-church evening service.

I began to hear noises in the hills. I asked a pastor near me, "What's going on?"

"Oh, the people pray here," he said. "They start praying on Friday at six o'clock in the evening, and they pray all the way until the service on Sunday. Every single week they pray like that — Friday night through Saturday night, until the service at 10:00 a A.M. on Sunday."

They didn't keep their prayers silent, either. I could hear a group over here, a group over there, and another over there. "The service tonight that you're addressing," he continued, "is going to be for the leaders only. The rest of the people are offering prayer for us and our leadership."

You wonder why revival is breaking out in Africa? You wonder why revival is breaking out in Argentina? It is because people are literally spending days and weeks in prayer. You wonder why Dr. Cho has one million people in his church? It's because, at any given moment, a minimum of fifty thousand people are on their knees praying. When government officials in South Korea were having problems with tensions in the street, they called Dr. Cho. Along with other church leaders in Seoul, he put together a prayer meeting attended by a million people. They told the devil to sit down and shut up.

Jesus said, when he marched into the Temple: *"My house shall be called the house of prayer."* He was not talking about the Temple. He was talking about a house, a kingdom that was coming into existence. The Temple had been relegated into a house of trading, forfeiting the power of God, negating God's presence to another era.

It is our era, the day when God's apostolic house overflows with prayer. The tragedy in the Christian church as a whole is that people do not pray. It's been said that the average Christian in America prays for five minutes a week. That includes prayer over meals and at bedtime with the kids!

Paul said, *"Pray without ceasing"* (1 Thess. 5:17). But can we learn to pray for even an hour a day? How can we exist in this world, with the powerful demonic onslaughts against the body of Christ and humanity itself, with less than that? "I don't have time," is the typical response. Yet if our spiritual survival depends on it, perhaps we'd better make the time.

It is a corporate calling, not just a task for individuals. So we must ask ourselves: What will make our churches into houses of prayer? I have seven suggestions:

1. *Experiencing tragedies and crises.*

Actually, heartbreak is often what calls us to prayer. Sometimes it is God's only way to get our attention. You see, because we're living in a Laodicean church age, and we are "rich and have need of nothing," we assume we have no need to pray. But it's a different story when trouble crashes in.

Listen, America: the Third World people know they must pray. There's no food for their children. They've run out of clothing, face sickness and disease, so they pray . . . or go under. But in the west, as a rule, we don't experience such obvious struggles for physical survival. We seem to think we can solve the other problems on our own. We have technology, after all. We have modern medicine and psychopharmacology. What can't we fix?

So God shows us just how much is beyond our control. We, too, are compelled to pray.

Naturally, we find the early church believers praying from the beginning:

> *And when the day of Pentecost was fully come, they were all with one accord in one place.*   —Acts 2:1

They were in prayer in the upper room, in the midst of an era of persecution, and the very power of God came down upon them. That's what it's going to take — a prayer meeting — to get the job done. Not a club, not some exclusive meeting of people who've been handpicked. It's going to take people who deliberately get together to pray. Through prayer, amidst all our tragedies and crises, God gives the power to break whatever is holding back the body of Christ.

2. *Setting aside the praying ministers.*

In Acts 6:1-4; Luke tells us that the church was growing, doing very well:

> *In those days, when the number of the disciples was multiplied, there arose a murmuring of the Grecians against the Hebrews, because their widows were neglected in the daily ministration.*

Then the twelve called the multitude of the disciples unto them, and said, It is not reason that we should leave the word of God, and serve tables. Wherefore, brethren, look ye out among you seven men of honest report, full of the Holy Ghost and wisdom, whom we may appoint over this business.

But we will give ourselves continually to prayer, and to the ministry of the word.

At this point, the apostles' role began to change. Can you see it? They began to move into an area of "extreme prayer" and ministry of the Word. They felt the pull toward social events as opposed to spiritual-oriented events. So they had to organize a group of men — seven deacons, who were Greek in nature and ethnicity — and separate these men to wait on tables. But the apostles said, "We are going to dedicate ourselves to praying and preaching."

That is what an apostolic house is supposed to be. It's supposed to be a place where you find men and women given to prayer and ministry of the Word.

Now I submit this respectfully: We have a great misconception, a designated job description telling us what a pastor should be. He is the one doing your funerals, visiting the hospitals, marrying the kids, baptizing, dedicating, and mowing the church lawn. But an apostolic house can't let the leaders be doing those things. They don't have time for it. If they do, it means they're neglecting the ministry of prayer and the Word. It's as simple as that.

3. *Having teachers who teach it.*

In Luke 11, Jesus *"was praying in a certain place."* His disciples came to Him to ask something of Him.

Think about it. What would you have asked for from the Lord of All? Well, of all the things the disciples could have asked Jesus to do for them, they made this request: *"Teach us to pray."*

Not teach us to preach.

Not teach us to interpret the Scriptures.

Not teach us to perform a miracle.

Not teach us to organize the church.

"Teach us to pray." No doubt it was because they witnessed something in the prayer of Jesus that stirred them to the depths of their being. It was in the way He prayed. In His posture, the words, the agonizing power that came over Him as He began to go deep in communion with the Father.

They wanted that. They needed to be taught, as we do. But is anybody teaching in your house?

4. *Learning how to ask for the bread.*

When they said, "teach us to pray," Jesus gave His disciples the Lord's Prayer. Then he said to them . . .

> *Which of you shall have a friend, and shall go unto him at midnight, and say unto him, Friend, lend me three loaves; for a friend of mine in his journey is come to me, and I have nothing to set before him? And he from within shall answer and say, Trouble me not: the door is now shut, and my children are with me in bed; I cannot rise and give thee.*

> *I say unto you, Though he will not rise and give him, because he is his friend, yet because of his importunity he will rise and give him as many as he needeth. And I say unto you, Ask, and it shall be given you; seek, and ye shall find; knock, and it shall be opened unto you. For every one that asketh receiveth; and he that seeketh findeth; and to him that knocketh it shall be opened.*

> *If a son shall ask bread of any of you that is a father, will he give him a stone? or if he ask a fish, will he for a fish give him a serpent?*

> *Or if he shall ask an egg, will he offer him a scorpion?*
>
> *If ye then, being evil, know how to give good gifts unto your children: how much more shall your heavenly Father give the Holy Spirit to them that ask him?* —Luke 11:5-13

Notice a key term here: *midnight.* Jesus is showing us that a midnight hour is coming in humanity when a journeying "friend" will need bread. The body of Christ has been on a journey for two thousand years. We have now come to the midnight hour, and we have found that we need bread. In God's Word, bread always speaks of revelation.

We have done everything in our power and our ability to hear from God. We have written every book on every subject imaginable. But it's now time for us to recognize that, as apostolic houses, we have to go to the friend that sticks closer than a brother at the midnight hour, and ask him for revelation.

Who's going to make it in this last day? It won't be the people who are merely faithful in attending church. It will be those determining in their hearts, "We're going to church, but we're going a step further. We are going to stick it to him at midnight and say, 'We're not leaving here until you give us some bread!'" We must have a revelation as to how we're going to handle the dilemmas of the human race!

There are millions of Muslims, Hindus and Buddhists, and in the middle of them all languishes a Christian church so fragmented, so divided, so sectarian! We are unorganized, undisciplined soldiers in the body of Christ. We're like the four lepers outside the walls of Samaria, begging for bread from a city where they were eating their children, facing an enemy that didn't care who lived or died. You see, it's time now for the remnant to rise and start calling for bread! In the Scripture we see three levels of bread:

The first level of bread is fine corn, or fine wheat, or a fine body that was brought as an offering to the Tabernacle of Moses. It was used as a wave offering to the Lord. This simply tells us: Our praise must be full-bodied, sincere, robust, and revelatory.

The second level of bread resides in the holy place where the priests would make bread with frankincense. It speaks of a combination of praise and revelation, in which certain bread was for the priests only. The priests would minister in the house of God, burning incense and eating bread from the table of showbread. It was imperative here that as the priests began to eat of this bread and minister to the Lord from this bread, that they walked in a new revelation as to who God was. Clearly our ministry must be centered in God, and revelatory of His truth.

The third level of bread refers to the golden pot of manna inside the Ark. It was a supernatural bread that stayed fresh, generation after generation. It testified that every single day God gave a new word. Every single day, God will give you a fresh revelation from His Word. Every single day, if you will spend time with God, you will get the true picture of where God is leading you. Our guidance must be revelatory.

Learn to ask for the bread. You cannot go where God is leading and calling if you don't have fresh manna from His hand every day.

5. *Purposing in our hearts: "We'll pray or . . . die."*

Is prayer your only lifeline? Without it, could you still survive? Or would your spirit starve?

In apostolic houses, people pray the kind of prayer that moves the devil and causes him to have a nervous breakdown. It's the kind of prayer that says, "God, give me bread or I'll die of hunger!"

"Give us this day our daily bread," Jesus taught us to say. He meant every day we need the bread. This is not a weekly request, offered weakly! And we can't just order our bread to be shipped overnight.

Such praying may not even be very pretty. Being a life and death matter, it will flow out mixed with blood, and sweat, and tears. In fact, Bishop Joseph Garlington says that his definition of revival is, "Snot." It's true, isn't it? When snot is flying, things are happening in the lives of people.

There's a story about the great baseball catcher, Yogi Berra. He was involved in a ball game in which the score was tied, with two outs in the bottom of the ninth inning. The batter from the opposing team stepped up to the batting box and made the sign of the cross on home plate with his bat.

Berra was a Catholic, too, but he wiped off the plate with his glove and said to the pious batter, "Why don't we let God just watch this game today?"

That is good theology when applied to the outcome of a game. It's terrible when applied to the way we live our lives and carry out the work of God. Worse than that, it is fatal. God is merely in attendance at the game of our lives, and our prayers are just a ceremonial function, a polite tip of the hat.xi

That is not the longing for bread of a starving man. It is certainly not the house of prayer God longs for!

6. *Being willing to fast.*

In Acts 13:1–3, a number of imperatives come through as we see the church moving forward:

> *Now there were in the church that was at Antioch certain prophets and teachers; as Barnabas, and Simeon that was called Niger, and Lucius of Cyrene, and Manaen, which had been brought up with Herod the tetrarch, and Saul. As they ministered to the Lord, and fasted, the Holy Ghost said, Separate me Barnabas and Saul for the work whereunto I have called them. And when they had fasted and prayed, and laid their hands on them, they sent them away.*

Look at this apostolic house, a house of fasting and praying. From that house the greatest apostle of all time was released.

I believe God is organizing men and women today who are going to spend days at the church, fasting and praying. They'll come and separate themselves for the whole day, just spending time in the chapel. Eating on that day will seem unimportant, a distraction.

When God begins to build an apostolic house of prayer, He will be looking for men who say: "From tomorrow, I'm going to start fasting. I'm going to gather with others and pray for at least eight hours. I'm going to pray that the house of God will be blessed, that its ministry move forward. I'm going to pray for people to be saved. And because all these things are so heavy on my heart, I just won't have time to eat."

7. *Letting our tears flow.*

Six months ago I addressed our church and said, "We have to pray and gather our tears. The Lord wants us to put our tears in a bottle."

I had no idea that a team in our church had already started gathering their tears this way. And this is a lot more difficult than it seems. But somehow, we got people gathering their tears.

Now we have bottles of tears that we are pouring out in different parts of our country. As we pour, we say: "Lord, these are the tears of your people for this nation. See us with our broken hearts, and come to our aid."

I'm going to bring a bottle of those tears to the United States and say, "These are the tears of the African people crying out for America." I'm going to pour them on the streets of Washington, D.C.

Until then, will you please pray?

7

OPENING THE HEAVENS: AN EXTREME ENGAGEMENT

I hope you're coming to see that an apostolic house, by definition, is an anointing God places upon an individual or a ministry — upon a local church or a group of churches, sometimes upon a community or even nations — with a mandate to accomplish certain things. The Bible says in Isaiah 10:27 that the yoke is broken because of the anointing. That is, the enemy's power is destroyed because of a level of anointing.

For many years, people have gone to church simply to appease their religious consciences. We can't afford to go to church for that reason any more. Rather, it is time to become extremely engaged with what God is saying and doing in the world. It's crucial that we be actively involved and engaged in spiritual things in the Kingdom. This is a level of anointing that actually attacks the gates of hell. And, according to Jesus, *"the gates of hell shall not prevail against it"* (Matthew 16:18).

Another way to say it is: an apostolic house should be opening the heavens. I want to explore that concept with you in this chapter. First, let's look at what happens when heaven is "closed." Next, we'll see what happens when apostolic leaders command an "opening."

When Your Prayers Bounce Back

One of the reasons God calls us to be an apostolic house is for us to open the heavens, even when heaven has become iron or brass. It will not be easy. For in various places heaven is closed up tight:

> *I will break the pride of your power; and I will make your heaven as iron, and your earth as brass.*   —Leviticus 26:19

> *And thy heaven that is over thy head shall be brass, and the earth that is under thee shall be iron.*

> *The Lord shall make the rain of thy land powder and dust: from heaven shall it come down upon thee, until thou be destroyed.*   —Deuteronomy 28:23-24

In Leviticus 26, the Lord spoke a clear and painful message through Moses. He told the people that if they allowed any form of disobedience he would break their pride. How would it happen? See the devastation:

> *I will even appoint over you terror, consumption, and the burning ague, that shall consume the eyes, and cause sorrow of heart: and ye shall sow your seed in vain, for your enemies shall eat it.*

> *And I will set my face against you, and ye shall be slain before your enemies: they that hate you shall reign over you; and ye shall flee when none pursueth you. And if ye will not*

yet for all this hearken unto me, then I will punish you seven times more for your sins. . . .

And your strength shall be spent in vain: for your land shall not yield her increase, neither shall the trees of the land yield their fruits. And if ye walk contrary unto me, and will not hearken unto me; I will bring seven times more plagues upon you according to your sins. I will also send wild beasts among you, which shall rob you of your children, and destroy your cattle, and make you few in number; and your high ways shall be desolate. —Leviticus 26:16-18, 20-22

Not a pretty sight! We put so much emphasis on where we come from in our religious heritage. We go back and date our authenticity as a people or a denomination, saying we were founded on certain movements, creeds, or religious experiences. But the Lord says, as we fall away from true obedience, "I'm going to break all of that, and I will make your heaven as iron and your earth will be as brass." Then, when we try to sow, nothing grows. When we try to pray, our prayers bounce straight back to us.

In Deuteronomy 28 the message is repeated. Dis-obedience makes the heavens as brass. In other words, it's going to be tight there; nothing's going to fall through the heavens. Prayers will not be answered; requests will not be heard. Your petitions — all of the things you're asking God to do specifically for you — will go no farther than the brass ceiling. You can fast, you can pray; nothing is going to happen.

I don't mean to depress you, but we live in serious times. If we are going to be moved to open the heavens, then some of us need to see just how bad it can be should the heavens remain closed.

It happened in Russia. There was a genuine movement of the Holy Spirit there in the early part of the twentieth century, but when Lenin and Stalin came to power, they made Russia a God-less place. When they became a God-less society, the heavens became brass over that particular part of the world. No matter how much people prayed, it seemed as if God wasn't listening.

I believe America is headed that way. Yes, we can walk into luxurious supermarkets and see shelves laden with goods — but that can change overnight. We can enter total economic disarray in a flash. It doesn't take years to bring about inflation and the severe loss of a dollar's value. In the last two tears, we have seen the value of the Zimbabwe Dollar fall rapidly; from 10 to 1 to the U.S Dollar, it slipped down to 17 to 1 and now it is at 5200 to 1. It happened overnight. Do we not take for granted our economic blessing? But if we continue to ignore the Lord and His Kingdom ways, we could be thrust into economic, social, and political turmoil in the twinkling of an eye.

Yet God is merciful and gracious to America. Wherever and whenever God sends revival in the world, there's enough money in the world to finance it. Much of it is right here in America. Because of that, we need to understand that when God puts resources in our hands, it is largely to empower and enforce the move of the Spirit by financing revivals wherever they are breaking out.

Will we refuse? Will we hold on to our wealth . . . and turn the heavens into brass?

Or will apostolic leaders lead the charge into opening heavens where brass has closed them up? One of our functions and responsibilities as an apostolic house is to go into the world and rebuke the spirit of brass so God can bless. I have been in places where, for years and years, prayers were not being answered, churches not growing. There was no healing, no deliverance, and no power. A social form of Gospel, preaching, announcing nice moral platitudes held sway. The saving blood of Jesus was relegated to myth, his cross effective only as a decorative architectural embellishment. How could God stand for that? Of course the church wasn't growing!

But there are places where apostolic leaders have commanded a better way. Through the Word of the Lord, and by authority of Jesus, the heavens have had to open.

When the Leaders Command: Open!

Heavens open when we command them to open. But it requires an anointing from God.

Let's look closer at this. Of the numerous apostolic types (or "leadership foreshadows") in the Bible, I'm going to mention just a few. One of the key roles of these leaders was to open the heavens. We see this clearly in Noah, Abraham, Jacob, and Peter. These men opened the heavens at some time or another in their lives. We must learn from their examples, because our function as a church is no longer just to get people saved and keep meeting on Sundays. We have a mandate to open the heavens throughout the world.

The Open-Heaven Syndrome is breaking forth in many parts of the world, even now. Here is how it worked for some of our ancestors in the faith:

NOAH

He demonstrated the magnitude of power. Noah opened the heavens by building a boat at God's command. The Bible says when heaven opened; it rained continuously for forty days and forty nights. That's the same magnitude of heavenly power, and rainfall of blessing, that God wants to send through the apostolic house today. God doesn't want to send just a sporadic shower, a move to touch us here and there. God wants a continual flow of His power among us.

Most revivals in the world last only for two years. The flame comes and after the flame goes out, the revival survives in the afterglow for about two years at most. We've seen such revivals in the previous decade; the revival comes but soon the flame dies out. The afterglow continues for a while. Clearly, we're not hearing so much about Toronto or about Pensacola anymore. The flame has gone out, and they're living in the afterglow.

God calls His apostolic house to live and minister within the great magnitude of heaven's power. Remember that the forty days aren't necessarily solar days. It could certainly refer to forty years of a flow from the open heavens where God blesses with power and strength.

ABRAHAM

He saw the fire fall. God told Abram to look to the heavens and count the stars. "So shall your descendants be," said the Lord — and a vast land would be theirs, as well. But Abram called for proof . . .

> He said, Lord GOD, whereby shall I know that I shall inherit it? And he said unto him, Take me an heifer of three years old, and a she goat of three years old, and a ram of three years old, and a turtledove, and a young pigeon. And he took unto him all these, and divided them in the midst, and laid each piece one against another: but the birds divided he not. And when the fowls came down upon the carcasses, Abram drove them away.

> And when the sun was going down, a deep sleep fell upon Abram; and, lo, an horror of great darkness fell upon him. And it came to pass, that, when the sun went down, and it was dark, behold a smoking furnace, and a burning lamp that passed between those pieces. —Genesis 15:8-12, 17

Abram saw flames from God, confirming that God's promises would be fulfilled, even when this man could see no rational evidence to support them at the time. After all, his wife would reach the ripe age of ninety — and still not a single child for them.

But then Isaac was born.

Later, when Abraham came to power as a leader in the house of God, he was an apostolic leader. And Abraham brought God down to the earth through the exercise of risky faith. He faced a fearful choice when God told him to offer his son Isaac on the altar of sacrifice.

Would he trust God or trust his own intellect? He moved forward in faith and opened the heavens once again. God provided. As rain fell by the faith of Noah, so fire and complete provision fell by the faith of Abraham. And Abraham believed God, *"and it was counted unto him for righteousness"* (Romans 4:3).

Churches in America need a real fire from God in our day. We don't need another great preacher. We've had all the great preachers we can stand! What we need now is fire, a heavenly response to risky faith, a provision from God when our own resources come to nothing.

We need the fire of God to set alight the vision of men and women in this nation. Then they will launch into ministries by a fearless faith, expecting God to provide, each step of the way. We cannot afford to function anymore without this kind of faith. Church is more than a business, a job, or an organization. It is a living and breathing organism whose life is the life of Christ, whose spirit is the Holy Spirit Himself, and whose Creator rules the cosmos. How shall we act any longer as poor orphans when we are the children of the Great King? Why should we not exercise the firepower of our position?

Yet we have done everything in our ability to generate a movement of God; now it's time for fire. It will come only from Him, at His time and place, when our hearts are broken and open before Him for we are saved by faith alone.

Jacob

He made a promise to God. Jacob ran from his brother Esau on his way to the land of Nahor. His journey was interrupted by the heavens opening, and he saw the angels ascending and descending on a ladder. Why did he see such a sight? It's because Jacob had angels in his entourage, walking with him, angels he didn't even know were there. His eyes were opened for a moment.

And Jacob awaked out of his sleep, and he said, Surely the Lord is in this place; and I knew it not. And he was afraid, and said, How dreadful is this place! This is none other but the house of God, and this is the gate of heaven.

And Jacob rose up early in the morning, and took the stone that he had put for his pillows, and set it up for a pillar, and poured oil upon the top of it. And he called the name of that place Beth-el: but the name of that city was called Luz at the first.

And Jacob vowed a vow, saying, If God will be with me, and will keep me in this way that I go, and will give me bread to eat, and raiment to put on, so that I come again to my father's house in peace; then shall the Lord be my God: And this stone, which I have set for a pillar, shall be God's house: and of all that thou shalt give me I will surely give the tenth unto thee. —Genesis 28:16-22

Heaven opened. As a result, Jacob made a promise — by faith — just as God had made a promise to him. Jacob promised to tithe from that day forward.

Are we sold out to God like that, enough to put our lives on the line? Or even our finances?

When Julius Caesar landed on the shores of Britain with his Roman legions, he took a bold and decisive step to ensure the success of his military venture. Ordering his men to march to the edge of the Cliffs of Dover, he commanded them to look down at the water below. To their amazement, they saw every ship in which they had crossed the channel engulfed in flames. Caesar had deliberately cut off any possibility of retreat. Now that his soldiers were unable to return to the continent, there was nothing left for them to do but to advance and conquer! And that is exactly what they did.

PETER

He invited the whole world. When Peter was preaching in Cornelius's household, while he was ministering, the heavens opened. He was lying on a couch in Simon the Tanner's house, and while he was taking his siesta that afternoon, the Bible says a sheet came down from heaven.

> [Peter] saw heaven opened, and a certain vessel descending unto him, as it had been a great sheet knit at the four corners, and let down to the earth: Wherein were all manner of four-footed beasts of the earth, and wild beasts, and creeping things, and fowls of the air.
>
> And there came a voice to him, Rise, Peter; kill, and eat.
>
> But Peter said, Not so, Lord; for I have never eaten any thing that is common or unclean.
>
> And the voice spake unto him again the second time, What God hath cleansed, that call not thou common.
>
> —Acts 10:12-15

Heaven opened to show that the church was open, wide-open to all. No person — Jew or Gentile, slave or free, man or woman — need be excluded from the grace of God. This Peter learned when heaven opened to him.

But what have you learned from the heavens lately? Do you want an open heaven? Don't answer too quickly, because when heaven opens, all manner of four-footed beasts are going to be in that sheet! No doubt your next move will come through what's in the sheet. So consider carefully: Can you work with those folks, many of whom will be "different," unusual, perhaps particularly unlovable?

Two apples up in a tree were looking down on the world. The first apple said, "Look at all those people fighting, robbing, rioting — no one seems willing to get along with his fellow man. Someday we apples will be the only ones left. Then we'll rule the world."

Replied the second apple, "Which of us, the reds or the greens?"

In his autobiography, Mahatma Gandhi wrote that during his student days he read the Gospels seriously and considered converting to Christianity. He believed that in the teachings of Jesus he could find the solution to the caste system that was dividing the people of India.

So one Sunday he decided to attend services at a nearby church and talk to the minister about becoming a Christian. When he entered the sanctuary, however, the usher refused to give him a seat and suggested that he go worship with his own people. Gandhi left the church and never returned. "If Christians have caste differences also," he said, "I might as well remain a Hindu." That usher's prejudice not only betrayed Jesus but also turned a person away from trusting Him as Savior.[xii]

When the Church Shuns the Sidelines

We hear so many prophets of doom these days. Media powers like Newsweek or CNN constantly report negatively about the Kingdom of God and the church. They predict that the church will not grow, that it will get smaller and smaller. But that is contrary to what the Lord says about the future. "In the last days," God said, "I will restore everything that has been eaten. Everything that has been stolen, I will restore."

Moses opened the heavens; David opened the heavens. Jesus, when he was baptized in Matthew 3, as he came out of the water, the heavens were opened to him. An open heaven is what we need in the world today. We have to see the handiwork of God in a way we haven't seen it before. I believe we are now going to see the heavens open and the promises of God come to pass. When God gives a promise, *"Let us hold fast the profession of our faith without wavering; for he is faithful that promised"* (Hebrews 10:23).

Why do we so desperately need this manifestation of God's power? One of the reasons is that governments around the world think we are trivial, made for sitting on the sidelines of history. They make major decisions for the nations without even consulting the church. Yet all of history is God's history . . . which is our history.

The world powers don't even think about us when making their decisions. Governments change their policies in mid-air because they weigh political pressure without considering the weight of God's will. They consider how much pressure pushes against a certain policy, yet there's been little to no pressure from the church.

The church has been merrily sitting on the sidelines. But that must change. What God is saying now is there must be a manifestation of the credibility of the body of Christ. One of the ways it's coming is through an open heaven.

Our children need to see and witness the power of an open heaven as well. In Revelation 2 and 3, Jesus comes down in the midst of candlesticks, and he shares church with John. They have church for seven church ages. Then in Revelation 4, John said: *"I looked, and, behold, a door was opened in heaven."*

Jesus was telling John: "I've had church with you for seven church ages. Now I'm going to show you what church is. And John goes and has church with Him — in an open heaven.

Intercessors of the apostolic house, when you pray daily, command the heavens to open. There's an open heaven coming, and we must give the devil no foothold to stop it.

A Haitian pastor once illustrated to his congregation the need for a total commitment to Christ that leaves no room for that foothold. His parable:

A certain man wanted to sell his house for $2,000. Another man wanted very badly to buy it, but because he was poor, he couldn't afford *the full price. After much bargaining, the owner agreed to sell the house for half the original price with just one stipulation: He would retain ownership of one small nail protruding from just over the door.*

After several years, the original owner wanted the house back, but the new owner was unwilling to sell. So the first owner went out, found the carcass of a dead dog, and hung it from the single nail he still owned. Soon the house became unlivable, and the family was forced to sell the house to the owner of the nail.

The Haitian pastor's conclusion: "If we leave the Devil with even one small peg in our life, he will return to hang his rotting garbage on it, making it unfit for Christ's habitation."[xiii]

Just as we must not let the church remain powerless on the sidelines, so each individual believer must let his light shine, and seek the greatest influence possible in the world. Leave no nail on the door of your soul. Allow no sin; allow nothing but a heart open to an open heaven.

8

POWER TO SEE, POWER TO DIG, POWER TO BE

Remember the ancient story about six blind men brought to "see" an elephant? "It's very like a wall," said the first man, as he touched the side of the elephant.

"It's very like a spear," said the second man, as he stroked the elephant's tusk. And the third man, taking the elephant's squirming trunk in hand, said, "It's much like a snake!"

"Nonsense!" the fourth man shouted. Stretching his arms around one of the legs, he concluded, "this wondrous beast is very like a tree!" The fifth man, touching the elephant's ear, cried, "Even the blindest can tell this animal is like a fan." And the sixth man, grabbing the tail, assured his friends that "the elephant is just like a rope."

Interpret the story as you may. But I glean this compelling point: It's very difficult to see something when you don't know in advance what it should look like. That's why we can thank God for our predecessors in the faith. They have clearly shown us what we should be seeing in our own day.

I thank God for the religious systems carefully placed together by the leading of the Holy Spirit during the past twenty centuries. I thank God for the evangelical movement that has brought us, as recipients of God's blessing, to this particular place in history. And I thank God for the Abrahams of old, the fathers of the faith, who have built an incredible Kingdom for God with practically nothing. Like Abraham himself, they simply followed in a wilderness, looking for a city whose builder and maker is God.

I have seen a poster used for wall decoration that displays a beautiful scene of nature — woods, streams, and a waterfall with the sunlight shining through it. The caption reads: "When I look, let me truly see." This is the seeing of faith that God gives us. It is our heritage from long ago, from the one who first truly saw as God saw. For Abraham looked and, by faith, saw long before he understood what he was viewing. That's how it is when we look at an invisible reality.

> *By faith Abraham, when he was called to go out into a place which he should after receive for an inheritance, obeyed; and he went out, not knowing whither he went.*
>
> *By faith he sojourned in the land of promise, as in a strange country, dwelling in tabernacles with Isaac and Jacob, the heirs with him of the same promise: For he looked for a city which hath foundations, whose builder and maker is God.* —Hebrews 11:8-10

Not only is it often difficult to know what we're seeing. Consider the chameleon who finds itself sitting in a bowl of M&Ms®. What color should I be now? We land in those kinds of situations too — where we don't know what we're supposed to be.

I grew up in a time when Pentecostalism was extremely unattractive to the society at large — and to some brothers and sisters in Christ as well. Speaking in tongues was questioned; walking down the street with your Bible was looked down upon. We were even called "cult-like" by some. But all of those things that Abraham did for us, we held dear to our hearts. If he could see God's blessing in the midst of the desert, then so could we. How could we let go of the vision, the city God was building?

Abraham is unique because he had a special vision and calling. He was able to leave where he was and walk into the middle of the wilderness looking for a God who spoke to him about moving from home. God said, "I'm going to show you a land, and there I'm going to bless you and make you very wealthy." Abraham had to leave the land and much of the family he loved.

When he arrived upon the piece of dirt called Palestine, what did he see? Lush natural resources? No. there was nothing that might make a man wealthy. But out of that useless piece of dirt God made Abraham a multi-millionaire. The problem is, Abraham had nobody to whom he could hand down his blessing.

As the years went by, God promised him a son. But when no son came, in a period of doubt, Abraham tried to help God out with a fresh-looking young lady from Egypt; they birthed Ishmael. But Ishmael, being the work of the flesh, was rejected. (Nevertheless, God did put a blessing on the life of Ishmael, because Abraham was a potent man in faith. God blessed Ishmael because of his father, and out of him came incredible men of valor). Abraham grew old and then, finally, received the promised child, Isaac.

When Abraham realized it was time for his shadow to start ebbing and for someone else to assume responsibility for a new era, the Bible says he gave all he had to Isaac. We might think of this in terms of material possessions alone. However, more importantly, he passed on to his son the resident anointing that was in him. There were little bits and pieces left for others. Abraham gave them gifts but told them they could not be a part of the next wave of

God's working. They would have to go somewhere else for their experience in God.

What does all of this tell us? There comes a time in your life when God has to separate you from among others. There comes a time when God selects a person and pulls him out, and pours something incredible into him. He allows you to see what's really there. He calls you to dig wells where once it was dry. He calls you to be what you never were before.

There comes a time in your life when you have to make a decision about who you will be in this world. Are you going to walk with God or are you going to walk with the world? The apostolic house is filled with people of faith who choose the God-walk. When they look, they see what God sees. They dig the wells God calls them to dig. They know the power of becoming, day by day, what God is making them to be.

> *Beloved, now are we the sons of God, and it doth not yet appear what we shall be: but we know that, when he shall appear, we shall be like him; for we shall see him as he is.*
>
> —I John 3:2

Such faith in God means putting your whole life in His hands. It's a dangerous thing! Because the pathway God sets before you may lead through much austerity. In fact, as the four examples below demonstrate, difficulty often precedes blessing.

Death First — Then Experience Blessing

Here's Isaac, a young man tremendously blessed. Even though Isaac received everything from his father, it was only when Abraham died that God actually blessed him. You see, Isaac had to allow his father to die.

Yes, there must be the death of a system, the death of a vision, before the new vision comes into full being. But we cannot perform spiritual euthanasia on our predecessors! We have to allow them to die a natural death; regardless of the anguish and pain they may be suffering. We have to allow the natural course of action set by the heavens for this individual, or this vision, or this particular move to die a natural death. And then we have to bury it.

Many preachers and many churches have thought they were doing the right thing in leaving a particular place or outreach, but they left prematurely. They performed an amputation and created trauma. They found they amputated something quite needed; there was nothing wrong with that vital organ when they cut it out. They should have allowed a natural death.

Only when Abraham died did God bless Isaac. Only then. And with the blessing, He said, "You have to dwell here at Lahairoi, " a place that means, *the living one who sees me.*" Isaac dwelt there for a number of years. At that point, his wife, Rebekah, was still barren. She hadn't yet given him the twins (who weren't much alike: Esau and Jacob). While the couple waited, they were growing, preparing for a new move.

Learn First — Then Do Ministry

When a new move of God is thrust upon you, the Lord may graciously give you a waiting period of peace and rest and growth. But don't take it for granted. Most often you'll need to study and learn as you wait. For example . . .

. . . you can't walk in the spirit of deliverance without studying what deliverance is.

. . . you can't walk in the gifts of the Spirit if you haven't learned what they are.

. . . you can't walk in a healing ministry by avoiding the sick and hurting.

When God calls us to ministry, He also calls us to learn, both at the beginning and as the years go by. So Isaac begins to learn some of the things that God is doing in his life. Then, only after a number of years — 20 years! — Of having a wife who couldn't give him children, he goes into intercessory prayer: Lord, my wife is barren. Please, can you give us a child?

Can you relate to Isaac at this point? Have you tried to bear fruit in certain areas of your ministry, but God is still teaching you who you are? Open your heart and mind to learn those things. Learn the associations and gifts he's brought into your house.

We expect children overnight.

We expect fruit in the spring.

We expect sunshine every day.

But God expects us to wait and learn. His power will make up for any lost time. Some of us receive a prophetic word that we're going to heal the sick, so we head to the hospital. Though the prophetic word and the faith to act on it may be right, we must learn what the prophetic word means. It may be five years from the time you receive the word before you pray for the first person that needs God's healing. Until then, wait and learn. I like how the great Bible teacher G. Campbell Morgan once put it:

Waiting for God is not laziness.

Waiting for God is not going to sleep.

Waiting for God is not the abandonment of effort.

Waiting for God means, first, activity under command; second, readiness for any new command that may come; third, the ability to do nothing until the command is given.

Is God calling you to do nothing at the moment? A Chinese boy who wanted to learn about jade went to study with a talented old teacher. This gentleman put a piece of the stone into the youth's hand and told him to hold it tight. Then he began to talk of philosophy, men, women, the sun, and almost everything under it. After an hour he took back the stone and sent the boy home. The procedure was repeated for weeks. The boy became frustrated — when would he be told about jade? But he was too polite to interrupt his venerable teacher. Then one day when the old man put a stone into his hands, the boy cried out instantly, "That's not jade!"xiv

Some things we can only learn through inactivity, waiting, and quietness. The Holy Spirit will speak the truth into us at those times, the times when we refuse to let our hustle and bustle squelch His voice. Haven't you found it so?

Famine First — Then Reproduce in the Kingdom

Some years ago in Zimbabwe, we suffered horrendous famine. Many starved, mainly because certain bacteria had crept into our nation. Like most bacterium it attacked the ecosystem, and was detrimental to the livestock and to animals in general. It also destroyed plant life in various parts of the country.

Then God permitted a drought — and the bacteria died early. This particular bacterium dies first in a drought, along with the very weakest species of plants, animals, and so on. Yet the very strong of the flora and fauna survive the famine and thereby receive the privilege of reproducing the new and powerful genetic strain of the next generation. This strain is so vigorous because it has weathered the worst of nature's challenges.

Do you see an application here? If you are in a famine right now, it's because God has created it and allowed you to be in it. You will grow weak . . . trust in God . . . and grow ever stronger. You see, amongst other things, famine actually purifies the soil. It purifies a particular environment. And the soul is an environment, too.

So the famine comes, and Isaac tests his blessing:

> *Then Isaac sowed in that land, and received in the same year an hundredfold: and the LORD blessed him.*
> —Genesis 26:12

He sows seed in the middle of a famine! Picture it: the middle of a wilderness, where there's no rain, no fertilizer, no nothing. Yet he harvests a hundredfold production, as a testimony that God is one who blesses His children. Because when God says something in your life, you can take that to the bank and cash it. When God gives you a word of who you are, and where you're going to be, you can be assured in the Holy Ghost that it's going to be all right. If God said it, you can believe it. But you might be hungry for a while first.

Get the Word First — Then Find Wells

Isaac receives a word from God, and he must have that word, that promise to proceed with his life in faith. None of us can afford to believe the lying vanities of things that the world throws our way, attempting to persuade us that God hasn't promised. If God has given you a word as to who you're going to be, and what you're going to have, better hold on: with Jesus you can make it.

Stay close to the Word of God. Let it become a part of your being. Immerse yourself in it, so that even at a subconscious level you are bound up with the Word — meditating, thinking, and dreaming God's truth.

The Word has great effect on you, whether you're aware of it or not. Consider a study looking into the effects of conversation in operating rooms. It seems patients under total anesthesia still have an unconscious awareness of the words of surgeons and nurses standing over them. Normally, surgeons have taken their patients' oblivion as license for talking as though the patient were not there — even making remarks that patients would find frightening if they heard. But two research groups report that what anesthetized patients hear can affect them. "What the patient hears — say a remark like, 'He's a goner' — could have an adverse effect on his recovery," said Henry Bennett, one of the researchers.

In one study, anesthetized patients heard a taped voice tell them during surgery they should signify having heard the message by touching their ears in a postoperative interview. Later, in the interview, the patients tugged at their ears, although none could recall having heard the message, nor were they particularly aware of touching their ears. Dr. Bennett, a psychologist now at the University of California Medical School at Davis, reports that when patients were given the suggestion during surgery that one hand was becoming warmer and the other cooler, the hands' temperature did so.

This suggests, says Bennett, inadvertent negative remarks — such as, "Wow, this is a terrible bone graft!" — could interfere with recovery. Under anesthesia, "Patients may be more vulnerable to upsetting remarks they might hear," Bennett says. "Their normal coping techniques aren't available, since they are drugged."[xv]

What we meditate upon, the things to which we attune our minds — even subconsciously — have a powerful effect. The Word speaks to our spirit and produces spiritual fruit. But our whole being can hear, and thus we must beware what else we tune into. All the other "voices" in the world also affect us at levels we may not have considered. Surely this is why the Bible says: *As a man thinketh in his heart, so is he*" (Proverbs 23:7).

God is creating an apostolic house. Our function, however, is not just for this house; it's for the many, many nations around the world, for generations unborn to come. When God begins to lead us further in that way, He brings us out of grief, ignorance, famine, and barrenness to know His Word . . . and then to do it. This is when we'll start finding wells of three kinds:

1. *Predecessor wells.*

These are the previous generations' wells, which we too must learn to drink from. We've got to drink from those wells if we're going to survive. We learn from, honor, and emulate those who have gone before us. God worked among them too.

But sometimes the devil will put earth in the well or curse what was begun. So we'll be wise and discerning when we're working and digging something that was there before. God may not want us to drink from a predecessor's well in such a case. Seek His guidance, moment by moment.

2. *Temporary wells.*

God gives us these refreshing drinking places to move us from point A to point B. God may position you in the most unlikely place and say: "This is where you have to dig a well." He'll tell you write a check when you don't have money. He'll tell you to go into business when you filed bankruptcy last week. He'll tell you to pray for those who are sick with cancer when you yourself struggle with disease.

God does those kinds of things, and He'll tell you that you need to learn to dig a well right here. God always invites you to do something you find uncomfortable before He allows you to do something you are comfortable doing.

God will, many times, give you a vision that will frighten you almost to death, because the vision will be so big and will encompass so many aspects of your life. It will pervade all of your life, your social circle, and your intellect. Your vision may span nations and generations. It will frighten you when you see what God is actually requiring you to be and what he wants you to become.

But He provides everything along the way as you begin walking in His will. Therefore, is it time for you to start digging where you thought you weren't able to dig?

3. *Permanent wells.*

These take on the nature and characteristics of the body of what God wants you to be, of where God wants you to be. When God brings a well into your front yard or your back yard, and requires you to dig, a number of important things take place in the house. People start walking in unusual prosperity. Missionaries from that house become empowered, traveling to other places — bearing gifts, not taking.

In all of this talk about digging wells, I am simply calling the apostolic house to be a house of faith, of walking by faith in every way and in every place. God is in charge of this house. When He says, "Rise up and go," then we go. If He says wait, we wait. If He says suffer the famine, we suffer with hope in our hearts.

We learn and grow, witness and preach at His command. We pray at His pleasure and perhaps even die in His Kingdom battles. By faith, all of our life is by Him, in Him, and through Him.

What better way on earth is there to live?

* * * * *

For if ye live after the flesh, ye shall die: but if ye through the Spirit do mortify the deeds of the body, ye shall live. . . .

If God be for us, who can be against us? . . .

For I am persuaded, that neither death, nor life, nor angels, nor principalities, nor powers, nor things present, nor things to come, Nor height, nor depth, nor any other creature, shall be able to separate us from the love of God, which is in Christ Jesus our Lord. —Romans 8:12-13, 31, 38-39

9

WHY BUILD THIS HOUSE?

Do you realize, fellow believers, that together we are a tightly framed, holy habitation of God? I can't think of a better definition of the apostolic house than that, straight from the heart of Paul in Ephesians 2. However, long before the apostle, when the great King David said he wanted to build God a house — a temple of physical stone — God said "No." Instead, the Lord would build a house for David, a dwelling place of God, which is not a physical building. The apostolic house is an amalgamation of the gifts of people in time, where God will release His will.

We're going to look at the authenticity of this house by reviewing some of the highlights in King David's life. For the prophet Nathan told David:

The Lord telleth thee that he will make thee an house . . . and thine house and thy kingdom shall be established for ever before thee: thy throne shall be established for ever.

According to all these words, and according to all this vision,
so did Nathan speak unto David. —2 Samuel 7:11, 16-17

David wants to build a temple for God. But God will build a house and a kingdom for him, instead. The temple will be Solomon's project, but the Kingdom flows from the original covenants with David's ancestors in the faith, and then through David himself.

Let's look at how God begins building. In Matthew 1 we read the genealogy of Jesus. Verse 17 says: "All the generations from Abraham to David are fourteen generations; and from David until the carrying away into Babylon are fourteen generations; and from the carrying away into Babylon unto Christ are fourteen generations." So here we have three 14-generation periods; from Abraham to David was the building of one household, from David to Zerubbabel was the building of another household. From Zerubbabel, all the way to Jesus, was the building of yet another household; three layers of houses being built.

The first layer was the Abrahamic promise up until David, which was a patriarchal anointing that brought Israel to the promise of inheritance. From David was the release of government. From Zerubbabel was the release of God's Spirit, as he said to Zerubbabel in Zechariah 4:6, *"Not by might, nor by power, but by my spirit, saith the LORD of hosts."*

Under the leadership of Zerubbabel, Israel was blessed to build a great temple. Antiochus Epiphanes destroyed this temple during the inter-testamental period called "the silent years." The rising of the Greek Empire destroyed the Medo-Persian Empire. Antiochus Epiphanes came to Jerusalem, offered a pig in the holiest of holies, broke down that temple, and destroyed it.

Then, a few centuries later, Herod the tetrarch built a temple for the Jews. It took forty-six years to build; being the temple Jesus saw when he walked the earth. But Herod built with blood money, so that temple had to be destroyed too. The Roman general Titus brought it down in 70 A.D. But when that temple was destroyed, another wasn't needed. Because the new temple was founded on the Day of Pentecost: the body of Christ.

Clearly, the house God builds now is not a physical building. We believers come together for fellowship and worship wherever it's convenient because the house God is building, is an enterprise of leaders and people. That house has foundations, it has walls, it has actual living stones fitly framed together, built into a holy habitation of God:

> *Built upon the foundation of the apostles and prophets, Jesus Christ himself being the chief corner stone; in whom all the building fitly framed together groweth unto an holy temple in the Lord: In whom ye also are builded together for an habitation of God through the Spirit.* —Ephesians 2:20-22

> *Ye also, as lively stones, are built up a spiritual house, an holy priesthood, to offer up spiritual sacrifices, acceptable to God by Jesus Christ.*

> *But ye are a chosen generation, a royal priesthood, an holy nation, a peculiar people; that ye should show forth the praises of him who hath called you out of darkness into his marvelous light: Which in time past were not a people, but are now the people of God: which had not obtained mercy, but now have obtained mercy.* —1 Peter 2:5, 9-10

Why This House Without Bricks?

Now why does God build this house? Well, as it was with David, so will it be with us. That is, the spiritual reasons God builds this house will come through in a brief study of David as we do some comparing and contrasting: David versus Saul and David versus Aaron.

1. *To establish rule, by the sword of the Spirit.* Here we'll focus on the house of Saul versus the house of David.

Saul's nomination as Israel's first king seemed an excellent choice. He had an anointing from God, and stood head and shoulders above the people, both physically and intellectually.

Saul's problem was that he had no one to teach him how to structure the Kingdom of God. As a result, he observed the nations around him for guidance. And we know where that can lead! Jesus said to his disciples that the nations build their kingdoms in a certain way, "but among you, it shall not be so." That is, do not structure my church as a secular kingdom the way the nations run their business. The system of man cannot regiment the Kingdom of God.

When Saul built his kingdom, he made no provision for God to build the house. One sad result was that, in his day, Saul allowed the Philistines to prosper as blacksmiths — which meant that the Philistines then sharpened all the agricultural implements and would not allow the Israelites to make weapons of war! So the Scripture says that in Israel there were only two swords.

Imagine! In the whole nation, two swords.

The sword is the power of the Word and of the intercessory prayer it teaches, held by an apostolic general. Saul held the first sword while Jonathan had the second sword. Saul was sitting under a tree, resting with his sword, when Jonathan went to fight the Philistines with his sword. But the rest of the army didn't have swords. So when David killed Goliath, he had to use Goliath's sword to kill this giant. He had to use the weapon of the enemy to kill the enemy; Saul, in building the house of God, had no mentality for equipping and empowering his people for the Word and prayer.

Remember, when building the house for God, put swords in the hands of the people. We have to be able to defend our territory and fight for what's ours. A New Testament church has to be excellent at interpreting the Word of God because we can only fight the devil with the Sword of the Spirit.

I was flying home one day and saw something fascinating. Looking out the window I saw a lot of paths on the ground far below me. I knew those weren't people footpaths, they were animal tracks. One of the things they teach you on a safari is not to make your camp on an animal path, because the animals function instinctively. If they're resting in the daytime, you won't see them. You can set up your tent, but then, at night the animals get up to graze and find water. Where do they walk? Right through your tent, of course!

They walk on the tracks they've provided for themselves. They don't just walk at random; they follow certain routes.

The same is true in the Kingdom of God. God has certain designated routes set up for us. Our steps are ordered by the Lord; there is a direction we must take. Thus the enemy knows where to set his trap ahead of us, seeking our destruction. He'll camp on our pathways — our seeming strengths and talents — and throw us off track. If we don't have a preceding Word — the lamp of God's truth to light our way . . . we're in danger.

David is our example here. He functioned on a preceding word. Saul didn't have a preceding word; he didn't even have a good testimony.

2. *To re-establish the glory, by worship.* Saul had no desire to bring the Ark of the Covenant back home. It reminds me of the little boy who knelt at his bedside on a Sunday night and prayed, "Dear God, we had a good time at church today. I wish you had been there!" Saul appeared to have no such wish. The ark represented the presence of God's government, God's glory. But it was left far from the people. In contrast, this was the first thing David restored. David knew the glory had to come back. In fact, the contrasts between the two men are shocking:

♦ Regarding worship. Saul had contempt for worship. That's why he once disregarded his office as king to do the work of a priest. God judged him severely for it *(see 1 Sam. 13:1-14)*. In contrast, David was a worshipper who loved praising God with all his might.

♦ Regarding obedience. Saul was totally disobedient to God's instruction. That's why, on a day when the Lord said, "Kill every Amalekite," Saul saved the king because he decided it would be the best investment. Because he harbored disobedience in his heart, he would not respect God's Word.

David obeyed God's word to the letter. When the Lord said to David, "You won't build a temple for me; your son will do it," David didn't sulk and pout. He simply obeyed.

♦ Regarding the occult. Saul had no respect for God's sovereignty. When things were going bad in his life, he went to the witch at Endor. He resorted to a psychic and talking with the dead.

Not one time did David bring the occult into his life. Yes, David had weaknesses, but he never aligned himself with witchcraft.

♦ Regarding leadership and human relations. Saul killed his strong men, feeling threatened by them. He manipulated and destroyed them. David never manipulated his strong men. He always had the courage to support and restore them.

♦ Regarding the holy. Saul showed no respect for holy things. He killed the priest at Shiloh. He had Doeg kill 85 priests. Yet David repented of even cutting the hem of Saul's garment, because he honored the position of king that a holy God had created *(see 1 Sam. 22:18; 24:4-7)*.

♦ Regarding "building the house." We see God building David's house but Saul not letting God build his house. Why you may ask? Because Saul is a type of the flesh. If we build by the flesh, we're only going to reap in the flesh. So any church or ministry built by the flesh, when the flesh is exhausted, it must die and will be buried.

May these stark contrasts inform us and warn us! The house is built for God's glory, amidst the worship and praise of His people. Beware the church where the presence and glory of God does not reside! Seriously ask yourself: Do I know how to worship the Lord? Do I engage in constant, God-honoring praise in my life? Is my house an apostolic house? True biblical worship so satisfies our total personality that we don't have to shop around for man-made substitutes as Saul did. William Temple, Archbishop of Canterbury in the 1940s, made this clear in his masterful definition of worship:

> *For worship is the submission of all our nature to God. It is the quickening of conscience by His holiness; the nourish-ment of mind with His truth; the purifying of imagination by His beauty; the opening of the heart to His love; the surrender of will to His purpose — and all of this gathered up in adoration, the most selfless emotion of which our nature is capable and therefore the chief remedy for that self-centeredness which is our original sin and the source of all actual sin.*[xvi]

3. *To disestablish old headship, by the new.* We've compared and contrasted the lives of David and Saul on many levels. We can see David fulfilling many of God's reasons for building his house. Now let's compare David and Aaron. First, realize that the house of Aaron was a limited fleshly order, ordained by man to do the things concerning man. A priest must be aware of the things of God and the things of people, because he must represent God to the people and the people to God. He must be an intercessor, or a mediator, between God and man. Aaron was that man.

> *For every high priest taken from among men is ordained for men in things pertaining to God, that he may offer both gifts and sacrifices for sins: Who can have compassion on the ignorant, and on them that are out of the way; for that he himself also is compassed with infirmity. And by reason hereof he ought, as for the people, so also for himself, to offer for sins. And no man taketh this honor unto himself, but he that is called of God, as was Aaron.*

> *So also Christ glorified not himself to be made an high priest; but he that said unto him, Thou art my Son, today have I begotten thee. As he saith also in another place, Thou art a priest forever after the order of Melchisedec. Who in the days of his flesh, when he had offered up prayers and supplications with strong crying and tears unto him that was able to save him from death, and was heard in that he feared;*
>
> *Though he were a Son, yet learned he obedience by the things which he suffered; And being made perfect, he became the author of eternal salvation unto all them that obey him; Called of God an high priest after the order of Melchisedec.*
> —Hebrews 5:1-10

Aaron was called of God, but he was only human. Therefore, his priesthood system was limited. He could do only certain things. In the Aaronic priesthood system, for example, priests couldn't also be kings. And the ranks in the Aaronic system were limited — some were priests of ordinary service, others would serve in the tabernacle alone, and others would be allowed in the holiest of holies. These were all limited functions.

David's order was that of Melchisedec, an unlimited order of priesthood. It had access to anything that God wanted. So God built that house over and above the limitations of Aaron. Thus, when the high priest passed an order for Jesus to be crucified, Jesus overruled that order when he rose from the dead.

Even though the priests said, "You must die," Jesus overruled that because his rank was much higher. Jesus, as our perfect high priest, is both priest and king, not limited to the human, but both fully God and fully man. His sacrifice isn't imperfect and temporary; it is both perfect and eternal. All this, connected to the order of David!

So understand this: Either man is going to make you his priest, or God is going to make you the priest. The choice is flesh or Spirit, limited possibilities or eternal salvation.

If I say to a man that he needs to be the next leader of a church, he will serve as an Aaron, which is a man-made system designed to accommodate man. But if God calls a leader, then he has access to the heavens.

A man-made leader has access to banks, but a God-called leader has access to government ministers. The man-made leader has access to the chief judge; the God-called leader has access to the Ruler of the heavens. The man-made leader has access to the Minister of Health; the God-called leader has access to the Healer of all nations, who died for us. The man-made leader has access to the welfare leaders; the God-called leader has access to the Almighty, who cares not just for human beings, but for the whole universe.

In our day we have a separation in the Kingdom of God. The systems of man who are building their own houses are separating from the systems of God who are building God's house. It is Saul and David. It is Aaron and David, the old headship and the new one. But on which side are you standing?

Becoming the House We're Called to Be

While looking at the system of God building the house, we are moving to the end; we are not yet God's house, but we are becoming His house. We're covering ground and we can see the end. We can see where God wants us to be, so we are in the process of becoming.

Let me use a woman as an example. When a woman is ten years old, her body is not developed enough for her to have children and sustain those children from her body. But at the age of ten, or eleven, or twelve, that young lady can see the ability coming as her body begins taking on a different kind of shape to accommodate what is coming. So before you are a mother, you start developing to become a mother.

Similarly, the church is now becoming a house. It is developing to become what God wants it to be and do. We are taking on the characteristics and traits of what is to come. If we reject this, we will not become the ultimate.

God is showing us that we are to take over cities and nations. We are seeing this in various parts of the world, such as South America, Argentina, Brazil, Colombia, and Central America. We're seeing it in Africa too, in Nigeria, Ghana, Uganda, and it's moving to Southern Africa. We're seeing some characteristics in little bits and pieces throughout Asia and Eastern Europe.

Leaders of the house are rising. Every house has a leader. As a leader now, if I take my house in the city and join with all the other churches in the city, I am the leader of my house; I am not the leader of the city. Each of the leaders lead in their individual houses, they are not in charge of the city. They only have charge of their particular house. But if we are going to take the city, then the house leaders must come together.

So God is raising up city-wide elderships, so the houses He is building are becoming strong. Houses that man has been building are getting weaker. Before David took over as king, the house of Saul became weaker and weaker. David's house — without even doing anything — was getting stronger and stronger. So that, when the time came for David to rule, his house was strong.

In like fashion, the systems of man are getting weaker and weaker. The systems of God are getting stronger and stronger. As these leaders of individual houses that God has built begin to rise, they have to learn to work together. The reason I use the word learn is that this is something we have not been taught to do. It doesn't come to us instinctively.

So each house in the city — even though it's an individual house — each house is being converted by the Spirit from a house into rooms.

On the city level, you're no longer a church! You're just a room in a big house. So imagine if one room should declare war on the rest of the rooms. For instance, if a bathroom says, "I'm closing," then we're going to have trouble! If the kitchen says, "We're closing," then no meals are being cooked, and we have to eat out. You know what happens when you eat junk food! If the bedrooms say, "We're closing," then everyone walks around sleep-deprived. So we have a house now, on a city level, that's totally out of order. That is not God's way. He is raising up the system of David: "I will restore that tabernacle again, with all of its rooms, on a city level."

Each of the rooms in a house that God has put together have to work together. A whole house is not a room. You don't cook and eat in the same room, you don't wash your clothes and dress in the same room, you don't play and study in the same room. A house has so many different rooms. So when your church moves to a city level, be prepared: you lose your identity as a house. You become a room. I don't care how many thousands of ministries you have in that church, you're just a room. This church here may have three rooms in their house, but when they come to this level, they are a room just like you are a room, with your thousand ministries and their three ministries.

That's what David did. He brought all the tribes, all the kingdoms together. Saul kept the tribes apart. David brought all twelve tribes together as rooms in one house. When he did that, God gave him peace from all his enemies.

Doing God's will. Having His peace. Doesn't that sound good?

I began this book by raising some hard questions: Why does the blessing of God rest in certain places and not in other places? Why are some church leaders more favored than others?

I hope that as you've explored the themes of these chapters, you've come to some very clear answers. I intended to explain and demonstrate the most basic, scriptural response: that God always blesses apostolic ministry.

Have you experienced this reality in your own relationship with God and His Church? If so, I'm confident that you also know God's most wonderful blessings. My prayer for you is that God will richly bless you, now, and in the days to come. Remember that there is no higher calling than to be a faithful servant in His Kingdom. It is a place of privilege and honor. If we fulfill our tasks with sincere hearts, relying always upon His grace for all our needs, then we will surely thrill to hear these words at the last day:

> *Well done, thou good and faithful servant: thou hast been faithful over a few things, I will make thee ruler over many things: enter thou into the joy of thy lord.* —Matthew 25:21

BIBLIOGRAPHY

i Listed as "Source unknown" at this website:
www.bible.org/illus/a/a-75.htm#TopOfPage. Posted by Biblical
Studies Foundation, 2003.

ii Basic definition adapted from Walter A. Elwell, Ed., The Shaw
Pocket Bible Handbook (Wheaton, IL: Harold Shaw Publishers,
1984), p. 346.

iii Today in the Word, June 19, 1992.

iv Story told by Mrs. Goodnight, quoted in Paul Lee Tan, ed.
Signs of the Times (Rockville, MD: Assurance Publishers, 1979),
p. 1261.

v Definition from sportswriter Bob Logan, quoted at
www.higherpraise.org/illustrations/vision.htm.

vi Lynn Anderson, quoted at:
www.higherpraise.org/illustrations/vision.htm.

vii Story from James Dent, in the Charleston, W.Va., Gazette.

viii Study by the Human Development and Family Department at
the University of Nebraska-Lincoln, 1983.

ix Annie Dillard, quoted in 2004 Christianity Today. April 2004,
Vol. 48, No. 4, Page 31.

x Lewis Smedes, (New York: Simon and Schuster, Inc.), 1984.

xi Berra story adapted from James S. Hewett, ed., Illustrations

Unlimited (Wheaton, IL: Tyndale House Publishers, 1988), 424.

xii Our Daily Bread, March 6, 1994.

xiii Dale A. Hays, Leadership, Vol. X, No. 3 (Summer, 1989), p. 35.

xiv Adapted from Haddon Robinson, Biblical Preaching (Grand Rapids, MI: Baker Book House, 2001), p. 102.

xv Taken from website www.higherpraise.org.

xvi William Temple quoted by Warren Wiersbe in The Integrity Crisis, (Nashville: Thomas Nelson Publishers, 1991), p. 119.

APPENDICIES

APPENDIX I

A SURVEY OF KEY OLD TESTAMENT APOSTOLIC MODELS

Throughout the Old Testament, we find models of apostolic houses and ministries. Jesus said you will know a tree by its fruit, so as we examine the fruit of these individuals and their houses we'll discover certain strengths and weaknesses to both mentor us and warn us. We will want to build upon their strengths and avoid their mistakes and failures.

I've put together this Appendix section in outline form, so you can easily refer to it as you consider your own character development and the progress of your apostolic ministries. Read these descriptions prayer-fully. Ask God to show you what, specifically, is here for you to apply in your own life and ministry. I am sure He will answer for your benefit, and for the spread of His Kingdom.

ADAM
began human history, but left humanity fallen

Summary:

Adam is the founder of the very first apostolic house. His life and ministry are extremely important.

Strengths:

♦ Adam was in a covenant with God and given irrevocable dominion.

♦ He was a dynamic organizer, caring for a garden probably 3,000 miles by 2,000 miles; he worked by a system.

♦ He was an awesome communicator: He spoke with God. He was very fluent linguistically, able to speak any language. The animals understood him when he spoke!

♦ He had unique giftings. He walked and lived in the realm of infinite intelligence, knowing virtually everything there was to know.

♦ He had no limitations other than the physical limitations of his body. But in his mind, he was the perfect man. He understood the nature and psychology of the whole earth.

Weaknesses:

♦ He couldn't deal with loneliness, something an apostle must be able to do. He noticed that everybody else had a companion, and he wanted one. And then she got him into trouble.

WARNING: Many ministers have fallen into sexual sin because they couldn't deal with loneliness. Learn to be with yourself and God, in peace.

♦ He lacked in spiritual courage, evidenced by his allowing Eve to manipulate him into eating the fruit without taking a stand. And even after the fall, by not training Cain in spiritual things, he lost a son.

WARNING: Many times, apostolic leaders can lose their taste for spiritual things and chase physical things like cars, and houses, clothes, and travel.

♦ He lacked godly parenting skills. After Abel died, Adam didn't bring correction to Cain. God had to correct Cain. But Adam should have corrected his own son. If my children don't live right, and I don't correct them, I put them into God's hands for judgment.

♦ He was a procrastinator. The period between Abel's death and Seth's birth is a long time. According to Genesis 4:16, Cain went before the presence of the Lord and accomplished great things. Out of Cain came the first builders and contractors, building cities municipalities, schools. Schools of architecture, schools of engineering come into being. And then there's Jubal, who dwelt in tents and raised cattle. So here we have the first agricultural systems beginning. Yet Adam is still sitting under a tree waiting for his wife to have another baby to replace the one who was murdered. While the world is moving very quickly in technology — in banking, in money, and innovation of all kinds — this apostle is procrastinating.

♦ He never took lasting dominion. God told him, "You must take dominion and subdue the earth." He did that before the fall, but he didn't do it after the fall. That is, when he made a mistake, he didn't have the ability to get up and take dominion. If he had taken dominion, he would then have overcome the curse. He was never able to deal with the curse.

NOAH
went where no man had gone before

Summary:

The Lord told Noah to do something no one else had done, to build something no one else had seen. He would go places no one else had gone. So he did it.

Strengths:

♦ Noah was perfectly obedient.

♦ He had powerful family values, demonstrated by the fact that when God told him to build the ark, all his sons and their wives got involved.

♦ He was a man of integrity. Because of what Noah had said in the past, his sons trusted him to build something important for the future, though it must have seemed ridiculous — it had never rained before!

♦ He knew how to make money; he was very wealthy. How do we know? Because he would have had to employ an army of workers to build that huge boat. Workers felled the trees, transported the trees, trimmed and shaped the trees, honed the lumber and put the ark together according to a plan. He had to pay them, and he had to have a lot of money to do it.

♦ He was a man of great patience. The project took him 120 years.

♦ He had tremendous faith. The Bible says, *"By faith Noah built an ark."*

REMINDER: If God says to an apostle, "Take the city," it takes faith to believe it can be done — especially if you're just starting and everybody else is ahead of you. Let Noah be your example here.

♦ Noah had persistence. While he was building, he was preaching. He preached, the Bible says, to convince souls to get into the ark. Nobody did. But that didn't stop Noah, nor did it change his message: The world's going to be destroyed by water.

♦ He was flexible in the midst of change. He had been working with human beings for a century. When the flood came, he would now be working with animals — all kinds of animals. He was willing to make that change and study animal husbandry. He had to trust that God would work with him in this. Then, when the flood season was over, and they came out of the ark, Noah was willing to start all over again with a new life.

Weaknesses:

♦ Noah lost the sense of his true calling. Once his job and mandate were over, he became bored.

WARNING: Apostolic leaders can become bored very easily, especially if they are between times of hearing from God. Noah got bored and built a vineyard. But he was never called to be a farmer. He drank his wine and got high. Because of it, he brought a curse upon future generations. *Read the story in Genesis 9:18-29.*

♦ He had an anger problem. The Bible says Noah cursed Canaan. Noah couldn't control certain events in his life; subsequently he then couldn't control the direction of his words. So he had the tendency to rage. He would blurt out and cause hurt. Beware: Any apostolic gift will have the gift of blessing and cursing.

♦ He was a weak father. Noah didn't help his boys in structuring correctly, in terms of the gifts that God had given each of them.

ABRAHAM

His faith was credited as righteousness in God's eyes.

Summary:

Abraham was often tested to see whether he would stay true to God. In the greatest test of his life, he was asked to sacrifice his own son in a fiery sacrifice.

Strengths:

♦ First and foremost, Abraham was a man of tremendous faith. It takes faith to be an apostle.

♦ He was a man of great vision. The Bible says he was looking for a city whose builder and maker was God. He was able to visualize that city and was actively looking for it.

♦ He could handle wealth wisely. He was wealthy as a coin merchant. When he came to God, because he knew how to make money and make money work, God was able to bless him and sustain his wealth.

REMINDER: In our ministries, let us not squander the money God puts in our hands!. Abraham had the ability to generate revenue and project revenue to the next generation.

♦ He was a ferocious warrior. He had 318 trained soldiers in his house, and they went to war resulting in many victories

♦ He knew his rank. That's why when he prayed, he prayed to God and with God. He made demands on God according to the level of the authority given him.

♦ He was a man of compassion. He felt for hurting people.

REMINDER: Compassion is the seed bed for miracles, even today.

♦ He was a team player. He could function well with various groups of people in his surroundings. He worked well with

Lot, with Abimelech, and even with Pharaoh. He never had a problem with Ishmael or with his servants, because he knew how to play on a team.

♦ He was a worshiper. He knew where to offer sacrifices and was always communicating with God. When God asked him to sacrifice Isaac, he was willing to do it as a means of worship.

Weaknesses:

♦ He sometimes "fudged" with God's commands. At times, he wasn't fully obedient to God's word. The Lord had told him to leave his family in Ur and go to a new land. But he took his father and took Lot with him. He brought the wrong people, and that hindered his blessing. Lot caused him a lot of trouble! Abraham tended to join with the wrong people.

♦ He could be an insecure man. When Sarah was in Egypt with him, he offered Sarah a deal. He said, "Look, you're such a good-looking babe. If the men start winking at you, just tell them that we're brother and sister." How amazing! On other occasions, he was very strong and secure.

WARNING: Many apostolic leaders want to be accepted and greatly fear rejection. Yet the Scripture says about our Savior that He was thoroughly rejected on our behalf and in our lives it is sometimes unavoidable.

♦ He was willing to take questionable advice. For example, "Why don't you have this child with Haggar? Why don't you divide the land and let Lot go this way?" He listened to unqualified people.

WARNING: Apostles may listen to too many voices, over and above what God is saying. Sometimes God will say a seemingly ridiculous word to you!

ISAAC
a faithful intercessor who couldn't make a decision

Summary:

This patriarch may have been a diabetic. He craved the meat of wild game, telling his son Esau: "Go kill something for me!" Also, he became blind very early in his life. Despite his physical problems, he was a man of faith and prayer.

Strengths:

♦ Isaac could handle loneliness. He was on his own most of the time, and in his times of meditation, he was able to develop into a whole man.

♦ He was a tremendous intercessor. The Bible says he entreated the Lord for his wife, and the Lord was entreated of him. Rebekah conceived twins as a result of prayer.

♦ He had great persistence. He sowed in a famine and reaped a harvest. Reminder: Apostles need not be swayed by obvious obstacles. When God calls us to a task, we can expect Him to provide all we need, famine or not.

♦ Isaac was a great builder. He opened the wells of his father and established his own wells by persistence.

Weaknesses:

♦ Isaac became isolated in aloneness, becoming a virtual recluse.

Warning: Apostolic leaders who have a lonely walk may tend to avoid rejection and become reclusive. Yet the Kingdom of God advances with relationships and dies when covenants are broken. We cannot afford to be out of touch with what's going on in our house and society.

♦ He had a hard time making quick decisions. Abraham could, Isaac couldn't. He agonized over the blessing for Jacob or Esau and then made the wrong call, because he couldn't make decisions. He couldn't even find a wife without his father's help!

♦ He didn't fund the next generation's work. Isaac didn't allow Jacob to build his household from the resources that Abraham had accumulated and that Isaac had built upon. So Jacob worked for twenty-one years with no money.

Warning: When the mother church is wealthy, it needs to provide for new works. Jacob had to start his ministry with no support.

♦ He didn't seem to be a family man. He and Rebekah didn't see eye to eye on many issues. That was transmitted to Esau, who was not a family man either. But Jacob, who was in Laban's house, became a strong family man, having picked up the good qualities of family life from his in-laws.

JACOB
a trickster who wrestled himself into God's blessing

Summary:

Jacob seemed to like playing mind games; he fooled lots of people. But he matured in the Lord throughout his life. Then, wrestling in the dark became the turning-point in his life; he gave God control. In the end, he became a great father of the faith, a good example of a worker and preacher who loved God.

Strengths:

♦ Jacob had a powerful, powerful anointing as a preacher. Could he talk! He preached a message sitting around a fire with a pot of beans . . . and con-vinced the entire congregation to give an offering! The man preached one message, and received a birthright. He preached to a woman at a well and convinced her to marry him. He had just met her. He preached to Pharaoh in his dying years, and the great king allowed Jacob to put his hands on him. That would have been impossible for anyone else.

♦ He was a student. He had the mind of a scholar. The Bible says that he dwelt in tents. The word *dwelling* in this context meant that he learned the culture of the tents. He apparently went to the tents of Melchizidek and learned how the administration ran there. He was always learning.

♦ He had a powerful mind. This was demonstrated by the way he positioned himself to manipulate situations. He even played mind games with the cattle! *(See Genesis 30)*

♦ He was a visionary. He could plan far into the future. We see this, for example, through what he imparts to his sons in Genesis 49. *"And Jacob called unto his sons, and said, 'Gather yourselves together, that I may tell you that which shall befall you in the last days.'"* He could see it all coming to pass, long beforehand.

♦ He was an incredible worker. Any man that will work seven years for a woman, without pay . . . has a solid work ethic! He worked fourteen years for two women. You always find Jacob working.

Weaknesses:

♦ Jacob would put his deals before his calling. This was his greatest weakness and would often put his calling in jeopardy.

♦ He was impulsive. How do we know? He should have said, "I'll work for a year, not seven years!" He just saw a lovely girl, was smitten, and agreed to seven years of slavery!

WARNING: Impulsive apostolic ministers can endanger their flocks with poor decisions. They must take time to pray and think . . . and listen for God's direction.

♦ Jacob was too emotional. Emotion is good, but too much is dangerous. His first wedding night, he discovered he married the wrong woman and he pitched a fit. He was emotional with Laban, with his parents, and with his sons. He cursed Reuben, cursed Levi, and cursed Simeon for killing those people at Shechem. His brashness caused trouble for him and pain for others.

♦ Jacob never recognized the gifted people around him. The only people he spent time with were Rachel, Joseph, and then Benjamin. But the rest of the gifted people — Leah, Zilla, his concubines, his boys — we don't see him spending time with them.

WARNING: Don't ignore the gifted people in your ministry, even though you don't seem to "click" with them personally. God will use them whether or not they become your close friends.

♦ He preferred negotiation over prayer. He rarely tried to solve his problems through prayer, on his knees, as Abraham did. He tried to solve things with negotiation. In his later years, though, he did find help and comfort in prayer.

MOSES
the greatest of the Old Testament apostles

Summary:

Who was greater than Moses? God kept him safe, even as an infant floating down a river in a basket! He was shy, but he led a nation of millions out of slavery. He had been a shepherd, but he ended up writing the first five books of the Bible. He was an introvert, but he faced God on the mountaintop and received the Commandments we must all live by.

Strengths:

♦ Moses was an intellectual. When he landed in Pharaoh's court, the king trained him academically. He learned all the sciences, all the disciplines of knowledge. Then he became one of Pharaoh's major builders. When it came to business science, Moses was absolutely unmatched.

♦ He was a military strategist, having learned this in Pharaoh's court. He fought the battles of Ethiopia, and then he translated that into his dealings with Israel.

♦ He was a powerful intercessor. God said, "Stand aside, I'll kill 'em all." But Moses interceded and changed the mind of the Almighty.

♦ He was a humble, meek man. But that meekness was not weakness.

Reminder: Apostle's ought to be meek. This is defined, not as a shrinking or fearful weakness but "strength under control."

♦ He was a delegator. He followed his father-in-law's advice and organized the people according to governorships. He was able to recognize gifted people and promote them to share his anointing.

♦ He wasn't afraid to confront issues. People did come against him — Dathan, Abiram, Korah. He confronted them and confronted Aaron when this priest led the people into idolatry. He was able to confront in the spirit of meekness.

♦ He was a spiritual man, always seeking God. He wasn't just satisfied with God's presence; he wanted God's glory. Nor did he try to function outside of the protocol set in his life. He never tried to offer the sacrifices, as King Saul later would do. That was a priest's job. Moses followed God's order.

Weaknesses:

♦ Moses had a bad temper that led him to murder an Egyptian, and later to smite a rock when he was supposed to speak to it.

Warning: Apostles must learn how to deal with anger. Even when revenge seems justified, remember that is God's work, not ours.

♦ He was a perfectionist.

Warning: Sometimes it's very hard to work with a perfectionist. In many ways, they're a pain. But we need those kinds of people to establish the bar. Study hard how to work with them in your ministry!

DAVID
the hero of all; a man after God's own heart

Summary:

David was multi-gifted. He was a man of God's heart, a worshipper, a musician, a fearless warrior. He had great strength; he was a giver, a man of tremendous relational ability.

Strengths:

♦ He recognized gifted people. In 1 Samuel 22, he could take all those in debt who were discontented, those who were discouraged, and could see their gifts. He could mold them into a tremendous army.

♦ He was a builder.

Reminder: Some apostles build and then destroy what they have built. Some apostles don't build. But David was a builder and maintained what he built. He built for his future in his sons.

♦ He was very honest. When he was exposed for what he did wrong, he dealt with himself honestly. He had the ability to repent and seek forgiveness.

♦ He was a poet. How we would miss his beautiful psalms!

Weaknesses:

♦ David had tremendous sexual weaknesses. Bathsheba: enough said?

♦ He was impulsive. He wanted so badly to take the Jebusites' stronghold off Zion, that he offered a deal that he didn't think through. He said, "The first guy who gets to the Jebusites, will be general over all my army." Joab, an ambitious man who didn't have a heart for David went and did it. Joab never became one of the greatest men.

Warning: We must think twice when we have an anointing. One pastor I know handed over his ministry to another in one service. A ministry transfer should take weeks, months, and even years. Not just one service. That's pure impulse!

♦ He wasn't a family man. He never trained his children. The kids were going crazy in the house. The one brother was a stepbrother and loved the stepsister. David never dealt with those things. Because he wasn't a good family man, he would not punish correctly. He would under-correct and over-correct. What Amnon did to Tamar was horrendous. He should have punished that boy. In addition it was Absalom who broke his heart.

SOLOMON
wiser than all; built God's Temple.

Summary:

Solomon started out with great wisdom, and was given the honor of building the Temple. But in later years he allowed his wives to turn him toward foreign religions. His reputation was tarnished.

Strengths:

♦ Solomon exercised wisdom from heaven. When two mothers claimed the same baby, he said: "Cut the child in half." The true mother thus revealed herself; she willingly gave up her child to save his life.

♦ Solomon was a great preacher — he persuaded seven hundred women to marry him! He got non-believers to give offerings to build the Temple.

♦ He recognized gifted people and he released them. He made great people greater. By doing that, he made himself greater. Solomon took a nobody and made him a somebody.

♦ He was a phenomenal builder. Beyond just the Temple or his palace, he built cities during his reign, not just in his own country but in other countries too. His kingdom extended from the Euphrates River, which is Iraq today, all the way to Alexandria. He built ships, warehouses, and storehouses.

♦ He was a man of peace. The nation didn't go to war in his years, but he was still a military genius and strategist. Nobody ever wanted to fight with him, because he'd already out-thought them. His army and soldiers were so wonderfully equipped.

Weaknesses:

♦ Solomon was an experimenter with other religions. He worshipped false gods when he became bored with the one true God. And he allowed his wives to worship those gods. That's what brought him down.

♦ Even though Solomon had hundreds of wives, he was not a family man. When it came time to hand the kingdom over, he hadn't mentored anybody. He was a great leader, but he hadn't mentored his sons.

♦ If you read the story of Jeroboam and how he was exiled, it shows you how Solomon could not deal with anyone who was competitive. He did not allow people to constructively criticize. So Jeroboam was sent into exile because he criticized the government.

♦ He apparently had sexual problems. In the days of Solomon, the Sodomites came into the land. We can't be sure, but there's an implication that Solomon may have been bisexual.

Warning: It can happen. Isolated and lonely apostles can get hooked on pornography, and that can lead to lustful forms of experimentation on many levels. Avoid this evil!

♦ He became bored quickly. Such people need challenges. Solomon ran out of things to do and build. How could he out-build the Temple? How could he out-build the palace he built? He had people coming to him from everywhere. What kind of a party is he going to throw next? When he got bored, he started playing with the occult.

APPENDIX 2

APOSTOLIC MINISTRY

The following are subjects pertaining to the apostolic ministry that should be considered in the process of growing your house into an apostolic entity.

"And it came to pass" – THE METAMORPHOSIS OF PROPHECY

Apostolic Call – Apostolic Choice

Apostolic chaos or apostolic order

Apostolic Character

Apostolic economics

Apostolic emulations: The origin of the Apostle

Apostolic evangelism

Apostolic Gems

Apostolic integrity

Apostolic Intercession

Apostolic Movements

Apostolic Offering

Apostolic Preservation

Apostolic Protocol

Apostolic Realignment

Apostolic Reformation

Apostolic timing

Giving birth to the Apostolic

Ministry: The Mentoring Process

Placing a demand on Apostolic Giftings

Preparation for the Apostolic

Prophetic Arts and Worship

Prophetic Consciousness

School of the Apostles

The Apostle and Spiritual Warfare

The Apostleship:

The Apostle's Creed

The Apostle-hood

The Apostolic and Liturgical Order

The Apostolic Mantle

The Apostolic power of words to form an image

The Apostolic Yoke-breaking Anointing

The Art of Visualisation

The Bishopric: An apostolic Dimension

The Gift of Interpretation

The Language of the Apostolic

The Mouth of the Apostle

The mouth of the Oppressed

The Office of the Apostle

The Push and Pull of the Apostolic Office

The Science and Power of Raised Idols

The science of Apostolic Attraction

The Sixth and Seventh day

Understanding the Apostolic Ministry

Walking in the Office of the Seer

Women Apostles

Your Mind Matters

APPENDIX 3

(SEE PAGE 8.)

APOSTOLIC GOVERNMENT
ORBITAL LEADERSHIP MODEL

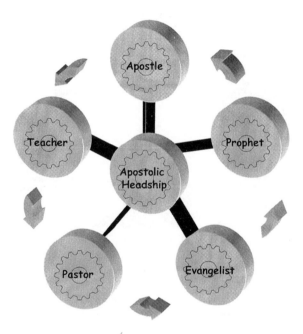

APPENDIX 4

(SEE PAGE 9.)

HOUSE LEVELS

1. **The Individual**

1. Spirit
2. Soul
3. Body

2. **The Family**

1. Husband
2. Wife
3. Children

3. **The Local Church**

1. Headship
2. Leadership
3. Membership

4. **The City Church**

1. City Headship
2. Local Church
3. Family

5. **The Kingdom**

1. Kingdom Headship
2. City Church
3. Local Church

APPENDIX 5

HEADSHIP, LEADERSHIP AND FELLOWSHIP

In Psalm 133, the psalmist describes as "good and pleasant" the state of the unity of brethren. He then proceeds to liken it to the dew on Mount Hermon, which is the spring source of the Jordan River which then flows down into the Jordan plane giving sustenance to a range of ecosystems as feeds into the Sea of Galilee before finally depositing itself into the Dead Sea.

After this analogy he then describes the unity of brothers to the anointing oil that was poured upon Aaron's head and ran down onto his beard and then on to his garments down the hem. It is there that the Lord commands the blessing.

There are a number of key points to note this picture of Aaron's anointing:

1. HEADSHIP: *The anointing oil was poured on to Aaron's head.*

The high priest was the head of the nation (the body) while the nation was a theocratic government. It was the high priest who went into the Holiest of Holies on the Day of Atonement and made intercession for the nation before God. He had oversight for the daily sacrifices and offerings. In all truth, if the priest was righteous before God (as Aaron was) the nation of Israel prospered. If the priest was wicked before the Lord (as Eli and his sons, Phineas and Hophni were) then the Israel was oppressed.

2. LEADERSHIP: *The oil ran down Aaron's beard.*

The high priest had oversight for the functions of the tabernacle, but he did not perform these functions himself. In Numbers 3, the Lord gave all of the tribe of Levi to serve and assist Aaron in serving the people as Aaron served God.

It is then clear that Aaron's role as HEADSHIP is to develop his sons and the Levites who are the LEADERSHIP. This role is two fold: firstly, his son Elizear was the next level of headship to ensure that the oil flowed continually, and secondly leadership, the Levites, had to grow in such a way that the anointing could flow from the headship onto them and then onto the fellowship.

Aaron achieved this dual, function with proficiency, while Eli failed In Eli's day the Bible records that the leadership, represented by Phineas and Hophni, squandered the anointing on themselves and them consumed the best of the offerings the people brought to the Lord. Eli, a the archetype of dysfunctional headship, did not correct his sons and bring order to leadership and thus left the nation exposed and his children could never serve as headship lest they squander the anointing that was intended to break the yoke of the Philistines on Israel.

3. FELLOWSHIP: *The oil ran onto Aaron's robe.*

When Headship and Leadership are in order and functioning as they should, God's anointing, blessing and favor will flow from them on to the FELLOWSHIP without impediment, and the fruit of God's favor will be seen in the fellowship as it is in the Headship and Leadership.

The best depiction of this is Jesus, Himself. When the women with the issue of needing healing, she only needed to touch the hem of His garment and she was healed.

When the anointing oil hit Aaron's head it transformed him

into a powerfully anointed headship gift that ordered the Levites in such a way that for all the time the children of Israel were in the wilderness God's favor was experienced by the entire congregation. The bible records that there was not one feeble or sickly among them, there sandals and clothes never wore out, they were fed food from heaven and watered by the Rock that followed them in the wilderness.

The house is in order then what is true of the head is true of the body.

The Sun, the Moon and the Stars

Another illustration to explain the diagram is based on the Sun, the Moon and the Stars as created in Genesis 1:14 and Joseph's dream of Genesis 37:9.

General interpretation gives the understanding of the Christ being the sun, the Church is the moon and the Saints are the stars.

A closer look at Joseph's dream shows that Jacob, an apostolic headship type, was the sun, Leah, Joseph's mother since Rachel's death, was the moon and his eleven brothers, (Reuben, Simeon, Levi, Judah, Issachar, Naphtali, Gad, Dan, Asher, Zebulun and Benjamin), were the stars.

When given application in our current discussion, the apostolic headship of the church is the sun, the leadership serving around the headship is the moon and the saints, the children born out of the ministry, are the stars.

In referring to Genesis 1:14, the sun, the moon and the stars are given for signs and seasons, and for days and years; and let them be for lights in the firmament of the heavens to give light on the earth to rule the day, and to rule the nigh. When cross-referenced this with Deuteronomy 4:19, then gives support to the idea that these entities are representative agencies appointed by God to serve heaven and earth, they are emissaries of God and not God Himself; therefore they must function in accordance with their purpose.

When the church is in order it gives clear direction to the world, interprets the seasons and prescribes the appropriate activities for them, understands the times and accurately states what they are and its light rulers both day and night.

In the natural the sun is a self sustaining star that generates light and heat for our solar system, and thus it rules the day. The moon is a satellite of the Earth and serves us by giving us light at night, thus it rules the night. The stars complement the moon's light. The moon does not generate its own light but reflects the light of the sun.

In the same way, Leadership serves to consolidate the rule of Headship. Psalm 121:6 affirms that when perfectly ordered the sun shall not smite the earth by day nor the moon by night, hence Headship and Leadership are not designed to smite or oppress, but to rule and guide.

The Fellowship, in turn, must shine, like the stars, wherever they are. In as much as the Headship is an exalted star in the church, the Fellowship must have the same influence on their homes, offices, schools, communities, cities an nations. In church they are submitted to Headship and Leadership.

APPENDIX 6

(SEE PAGE 46.)

THE WHEEL WITHIN THE WHEEL
APOSTOLIC HEADSHIP & LEADERSHIP

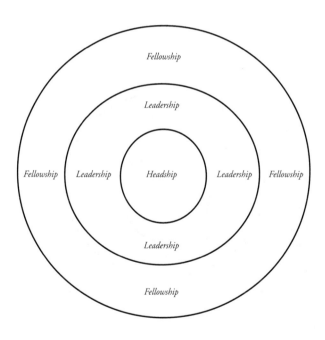

APPENDIX 7

(SEE PAGE 46.)

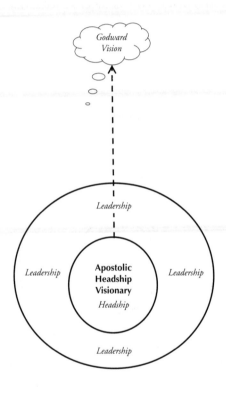

Appendix 8

(See Page 46.)

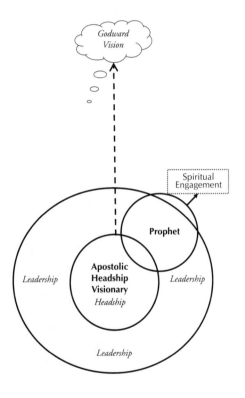

APPENDIX 9

(SEE PAGE 46.)

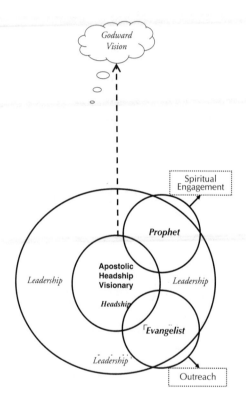

APPENDIX **10**

(SEE PAGE 46.)

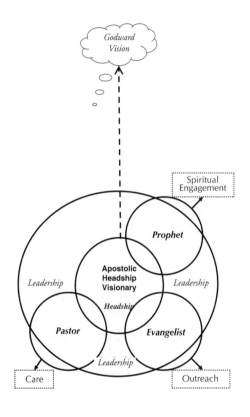

Appendix 11

(See Page 46.)

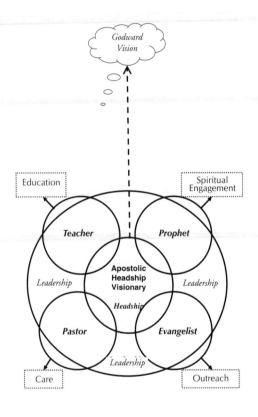

APPENDIX 12

(SEE PAGE 46.)

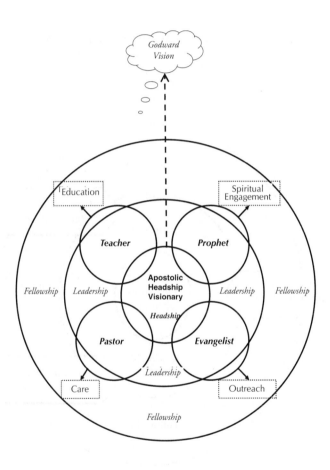

APPENDIX 13

(SEE PAGE 46.)

APOSTOLIC GOVERNMENT — THE APOSTLE

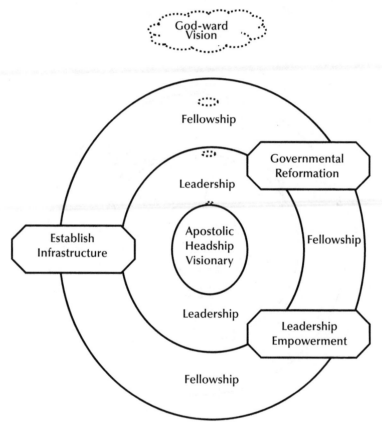

APPENDIX 14

(SEE PAGE 46.)

APOSTOLIC GOVERNMENT — THE PROPHET

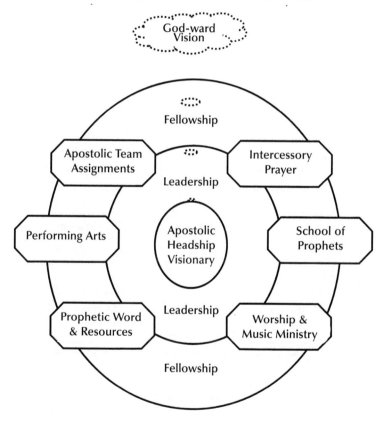

APPENDIX 15

(SEE PAGE 46.)

APOSTOLIC GOVERNMENT — THE EVANGELIST

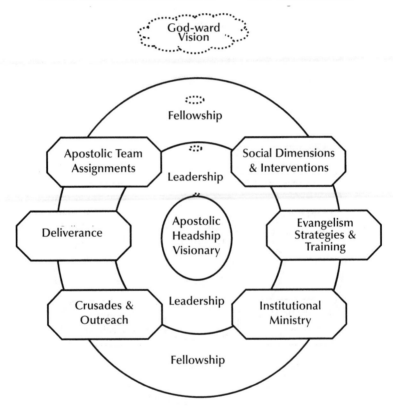

APPENDIX 16

(SEE PAGE 46.)

APOSTOLIC GOVERNMENT — THE PASTOR

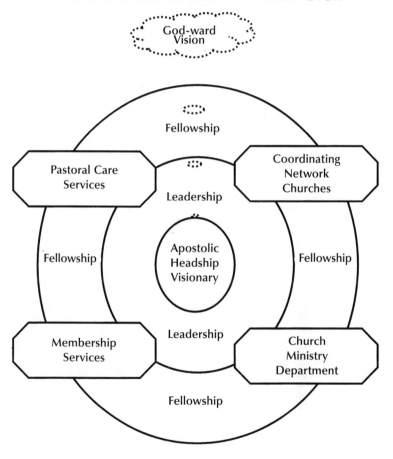

APPENDIX 17

(SEE PAGE 46.)

APOSTOLIC GOVERNMENT — THE TEACHER

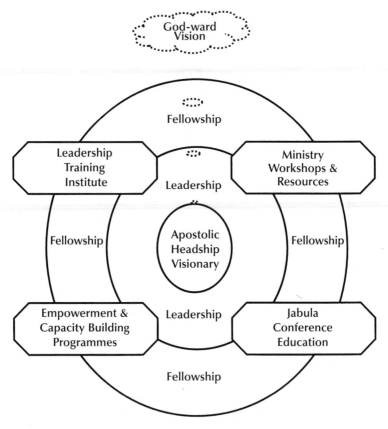

APPENDIX 18

(SEE PAGE 46.)

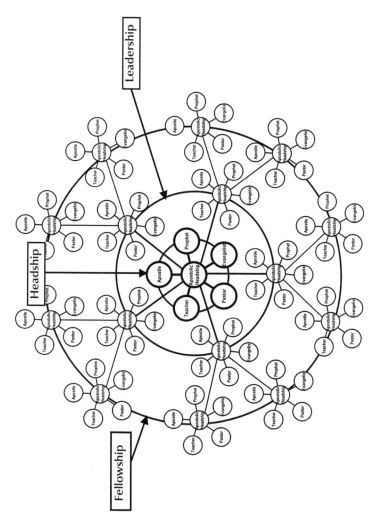

APOSTOLIC GOVERNMENT — THE WHEEL WITHIN THE WHEEL

COVENANT PARTNER INFORMATION

Dear Friend,

Thank you for taking the time to take a closer look at Jabula –
New Life Ministries. While our ministry is taking us to the
United States, Canada, the United Kingdom, and other nations
around the world, we are endeavoring to answer the call of God
in our homeland of Africa. God has given us a specific mandate
to EMPOWER the people of Africa, by providing for them in a
number of areas. Truly God is blessing in unprecedented ways,
but at the same time, the needs of people are growing, the costs
to bring this needed help are escalating, and our economy at
home is in absolute demise. We must depend on the support of
our friends in the United States and Europe to empower us to
continue these efforts.

I want to personally ask you to prayerfully consider becoming a
Covenant Partner with us on a financial level. As you covenant
together with us for this Kingdom mandate, we believe that you
become a part of God's blessing as well. Thank you in advance
for your role in helping answer the call of God. May God richly
bless you, and open the windows of heaven over you life!

Sincerely,

Bishop Tudor Bismark

Below is a basic outline of what God has called us to accomplish for His glory.

JABULA MEDICAL PROGRAM

• Medical Mobile Clinic

• Ambulances for Emergency Transfers

• Seeing between 1,000 to 1,500 Weekly

• A wide range of diseases (HIV, Cholera, TB, Skin issues, etc.)

• Medical/Hygiene packets

ORPHAN RELIEF AND ASSISTANCE

• One in four Zimbabweans is an orphan

• Currently providing for over 100 children

• Provide housing (build orphanage facilities)

• Provide food, clothing, and medical care

• Provide educational assistance

Education Program (Jabula Foundation)

- Currently providing education assistance to over 2,500 children

- Provide teachers' salaries

- Build schools and classrooms

- Provide books and supplies

- Commitment through college degree

Widows/Elderly Care

- Caring for over 3,000 widows and elderly

- Provide housing (build living facilities)

- Provide food, clothing, and medical care

Ministry/Pastors Support

- Provide covering to over 1,000 pastors

- Operate Bible schools in several locations

- Provide monthly financial support for over 200 pastors

- Provide regional conference to train and empower

RESOURCES

TAPE SERIES

The preeminence of the Kingdom at this time cannot be denied or ignored. God is indeed calling His church back to their rightful role and function in the earth. Contained in these messages are powerful principles and concepts as to the way the Kingdom of God is functioning in the earth today. As you engage the process of learning this material, we believe that you will be changed and transformed into the person that God intended you to be in the beginning of time. Welcome to the Kingdom!

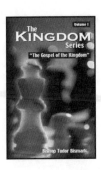

The Kingdom Series Volume I
"The Gospel of the Kingdom"

Tape One   *Kingdom I*

Tape Two   *Kingdom II*

Tape Three   *Kingdom III*

Tape Four   *Kingdom Aggression*

Tape Five   *The Might of God*

The Kingdom Series Volume II
"Kingdom Dominion"

Tape One   *Kingdom Dominion I*

Tape Two   *Kingdom Dominion II*

Tape Three   *Kingdom Dominion III*

Tape Four   *Kingdom Dominion IV*

The Kingdom Series   Volume III
"The Kingdom Mindset"
Tape One   *Your Legal Rights I*
Tape Two   *Your Legal Rights II*
Tape Three   *Your Legal Rights III*
Tape Four   *Kingdom Authority - Healing*

The Kingdom Series   Volume IV
"Kingdom Resurrection"
Tape One   *Kingdom Resurrection I*
Tape Two   *Kingdom Resurrection II*
Tape Three   *Kingdom Resurrection III*
Tape Four   *Kingdom Resurrection IV*

Kingdom Series   Volume V
"Wisdom and Judgement"
Tape One   *Kingdom Wisdom*
Tape Two   *Commit Your Thoughts*
Tape Three   *Lawgiver I*
Tape Four   *Lawgiver II*

The Nature of the Beast

Tape One   *The Nature of the Beast*

Tape Two   *Breaking The Nature of the Beast*

When mankind fell, we were thrust into the arena of the nature and manifestation of the Antichrist, which in this series we are calling "The Nature of the Beast. These teachings are designed to help you to understand how Jesus Christ and His Church, together, reverse this equation and releases us into the Kingdom restored to His image.

The Spirit of the "Ites"

Tape One   *The Spirit of the "Ites"*

Tape Two   *The Spirit of the "Ites" II*

When the Children of Israel took the land of Canaan, they found and learned a number of things, one of which was what we refer to as the "The Ites". This was organized group of nations designed as a system to oppose Israel. These same systems exist in our world today, and are being used by Satan to hinder development and progress of God's church. This series deals with how to identify and how to be liberated from "The Spirit of the Ites".

Blessed, Beyond The Curse!

Tape One   *The Generational Blessing*

Tape Two   *Blessed Enough to Break The Curse*

Tape Three   *The Curse Can't Hold Me*

As sons of God, we have a destiny that requires us to be blessed. It is Satan's desire to interfere with this release, and impose curses on our lives and ministries. In this series, we deal with the process of coming out of curse oriented conditions and organized demonic schemes, into a sphere of blessing and freedom. I am blessed and NOT cursed!

Breakthrough Anointing

Tape One   *Children In The Marketplace*

Tape Two   *A Ridiculous Blessing*

Tape Three   *Kick That Door Open*

Immaturity is one of the greatest INHIBITING factors in the Body of Christ today. Hebrews 6:1-2 reveals that we are to move on to perfection; a state where we can be trusted with "True" riches. In this series, we learn that God desires to systematically grow us, so that we are positioned to receive the fullness and the magnitude of God's release in our lives.

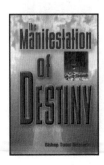

Manifestation of Destiny

Tape One	*The Manifestation of Destiny I*
Tape Two	*The Manifestation of Destiny II*
Tape Three	*Manifestation Destroys the Works of the Enemy*
Tape Four	*The Fourth Dimension of Revelation*

Everything that takes place the earthly or physical realm, happens first in the heavenlies. Eccl 3:14 & Acts 15: 18 declare that all decisions were made in eternity before the world began. This series will elevate your faith and ability to step into the manifestation of what is already established in heaven as relates to your life.

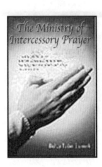

The Ministry of Intercessory Prayer

Tape One	*Intercessory Prayer*
Tape Two	*Intercessory Prayer — Taking Cities*

We are living in the day of the greatest prayer movement that has ever been seen in the history of mankind. The number of Christians praying today far exceeds the total number of believers that have prayed in preceding centuries and millenia.

Government and Order

Tape One   *Basic Church Government*

Tape Two   *Kingdom Government*

Tape Three   *Kingdom Structure*

Tape Four   *Headship*

Tape Five   *Thy Kingdom Come*

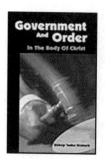

In the last days, God said he would rebuild the Tabernacle of David. This is the re-establishing of the Government of God. In this series you will learn principles like: Basic Church Government; Kingdom Government; Restoring Order; and more.

Breaking Curses

Tape One   *Breaking Curses Part 1*

Tape Two   *Breaking Curses Part 2*

Tape Three   *The Blessing*

Tape Four   *The Bastard Curse*

Are you continually encumbered with sickness, financial bon-dage, temptation, or poor relationships? Do you feel like you will never break through? Learn how to be free from issues you thought you had to live with!

The Anointing of an Apostolic House

Tape One *House of Prayer*

Tape Two *House of Deliverance*

Tape Three *Opening the Heavens*

Tape Four *Power To Dig Wells*

Tape Five *Measure of Rule*

God is establishing and raising up Apostolic Houses which will bring order and government back to His Kingdom. In this series, learn some of the key characteristics of Apostolic Houses.

BOOKS

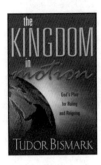

The Kingdom in Motion

In *The Kingdom in Motion*, Bishop Tudor Bismark carefully unfolds key passages in the Gospel of Matthew, demonstrating how the ancient promises are coming to fruition in our day. The time has come when all Christians must become "Kingdom bearers," to rule and reign with Him!

The Anointing of a Thousand Times More

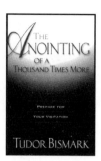

This book will open your eyes to the power of God's anointing and will show you practical ways to prepare for this impartation. God is awakening the Church to be life changers, city changers, and world changers.

Order in the House

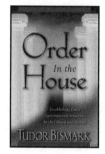

In this compelling book, Bishop Tudor Bismark opens the Word of God and the way it unfolds according to the specific governmental order as relayed in Scripture. We must understand and walk in "order" if we are to experience all the benefits of Kingdom living. *Order in the House* is God's call to every believer and every church in this season. Are you listening, and will you answer the call?

For more information or to send a donation, please visit one of our websites:

www.jabula.org

or

www.tudorbismark.org

or contact us:

United States
Jabula-New Life Ministries
445 E. FM 1382, Suite 3-371
Cedar Hill, Texas 75104

(800) 671-0844
(469) 272-7337

E-Mail:
info@jabula.org
or
info@tudorbismark.org

NOTES

NOTES

NOTES

NOTES

NOTES

NOTES

NOTES

NOTES

NOTES

NOTES

NOTES

NOTES